Presented To:

_____

From:

_____

Date:

_____

Praying Your Way to a Beautiful Life

Daily Prayers for Women

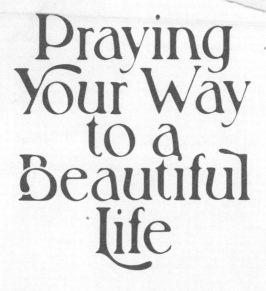

Praying Your Way to a Beautiful Life

Daily Prayers for Women

BARBOUR
PUBLISHING

Introduction

If you crave a life full of hope and beauty. . .this book of daily prayers is just what your heart needs!

This book of inspirational daily prayers will set you on a path to beautiful living. Each devotional-like prayer and related scripture selection will help you to discover compassion and grace, calm and contentment, confidence and strength, and so much more, every day of the year! Between the pages of this book, you'll embrace a life of purpose with the heavenly Father as your friend and guide.

A truly beautiful life. . .is just a prayer away!

Day 1

Patterned after Christ

Lord, I want to be like You. I want to have that calm that radiates from Your presence. I want to have that peace of mind that flows like a river, never stagnant but calmly streaming its way into the hearts of all who follow You. Show me how not to worry. Help me remember that You know how many strands of hair are on my head, that You see, that You know what I need before I need it. Help me get it through my head that no matter how hard the earth shakes or how often mountains fall into the sea, You will be watching over me, keeping me safe. Remind me, Lord, that with You in my life, I can walk tall because I will lack nothing. Help me to rest secure, knowing that even when I fall asleep, You will remain with me, guarding my thoughts, holding me close, and reassuring me when I'm frightened. Help me become so secure in You that I too can walk on water and move mountains. In Your name I pray, amen.

Pattern yourselves after me [follow my example],
as I imitate and follow Christ (the Messiah).

1 CORINTHIANS 11:1 AMPC

Day 2

Truth over Intimidation

Dear God, I am intimidated by so many people. It seems like everyone makes me feel inferior because I see them as better than me. I believe they matter more. Why do I always think that way? I know that You made me on purpose, so why don't I see my worth? I'm afraid I'll always feel less than others because of the way I look, the way I act, or a million other things. Give me the courage to believe I am who You say I am. Help me stand strong in the truth that I'm made on purpose and for a purpose. Make me brave enough to believe I have value and worth because of who I am on the inside. In Jesus' name I pray, amen.

"Be strong. Take courage. Don't be intimidated. Don't give them a second thought because GOD, *your God, is striding ahead of you. He's right there with you. He won't let you down; he won't leave you."*

DEUTERONOMY 31:6 MSG

Day 3

Like a Little Child

Help me, Lord, to become more like a little child. For I know that when I trust in You, depending on You for every need and desire, my worries will wane.

So keep me as humble, simple, modest, meek, and forgiving as a child, Lord. Make me a more accepting and curious person, one who looks for and expects only the good in all things and all people. Lastly, Lord, lift me up into Your arms when I come running to You with all my troubles, worries, woes, and tears, looking to You for solace, affection, and answers to all my *why* questions.

I ask all these things, knowing that the more I become like that little child You created me to be—more trusting, loving, and forgiving—the closer I will be to Your kingdom in heaven. In Jesus' name I pray, amen.

Truly I say to you, unless you repent (change, turn about) and become like little children [trusting, lowly, loving, forgiving], you can never enter the kingdom of heaven [at all]. Whoever will humble himself therefore and become like this little child [trusting, lowly, loving, forgiving] is greatest in the kingdom of heaven.
MATTHEW 18:3–4 AMPC

Day 4

Pray Your Worries Away

Lord, I'm wringing my hands again. But I know where to turn with my worries—to Your Word. I've come seeking answers, a divine easing to my mercurial stress levels that spike the moment my feet dangle over the heat of another tough day, a bad decision, strained finances, illness, or a wayward child. And in this verse I find hope: pray about everything. *Every little thing.*

If I believe You are the Big Deal, the Creator of this glorious universe—the Creator of *me*—then I must believe You've got this. How very arrogant of me to think that my problems could ever be Your final straw. God, I commit to asking what *You* think about everything happening in my life. Every. Little. Thing. Because You've got this. Amen.

Don't worry about anything, but in everything, through prayer
and petition with thanksgiving, present your requests to God.
And the peace of God, which surpasses all understanding,
will guard your hearts and minds in Christ Jesus.

PHILIPPIANS 4:6–7 CSB

Day 5

Fundamental Fact of Faith

Lord, You are the one who makes my life worth living. For You give me the hope I crave and the provision I need. This faith I have in You is my foundation, the rock that helps me weather the storms that come my way.

My faith is the same faith that helped those who've gone before, ones who courageously traveled into unknown territories, knowing You would be with them, help them, guide them every step of the way.

May that same faith help me see there is more beyond my mortal vision. For You have created and continually will create the visible out of the invisible. And with that power at Your command, I need not fear nor fret nor worry about anything. That's the fundamental fact of faith. In Jesus' name, amen.

The fundamental fact of existence is that this trust in God, this faith, is the firm foundation under everything that makes life worth living. It's our handle on what we can't see. The act of faith is what distinguished our ancestors, set them above the crowd. By faith, we see the world called into existence by God's word, what we see created by what we don't see.

HEBREWS 11:1–3 MSG

Day 6

Strength in Convictions

Dear God, it's hard to hold on to my convictions in today's world. It feels like society is working overtime to demoralize me for my values, making me feel irrelevant. They preach blatant immorality, and when anyone stands up against it, that person is blasted. I'm fearful to speak up. Inside I may hold my convictions tight, but I'm afraid to speak them out loud. I don't want to live my one and only life shut down like that. And I know it's not how You intended me to live either. I want my life to point others to You in heaven. Let my words and actions make a strong case for being a Christ follower. In Jesus' name I pray, amen.

Keep your eyes open, hold tight to your convictions,
give it all you've got, be resolute, and love without stopping.
1 CORINTHIANS 16:13–14 MSG

Day 7

Stayed on God

I know I'm in trouble, Lord, when my thoughts ricochet around in my head, jumping from fretfulness to fear and back again. Help me rein in my thoughts, Lord. Help me focus all my faculties on You, Your love, Your power, Your joy, Your peace. Help me to commit myself to You, knowing You are the steady and everlasting rock on which I can rely. Show me how to lean on You and hope in You, confidently knowing You are the one I can trust to guide me in the right direction. You are the good shepherd who can and will care for me when I need strength, support, comfort, protection, and provision. In Jesus' name I live, and breathe, and pray, amen.

You will guard him and keep him in perfect and constant peace whose mind [both its inclination and its character] is stayed on You, because he commits himself to You, leans on You, and hopes confidently in You. So trust in the Lord (commit yourself to Him, lean on Him, hope confidently in Him) forever; for the Lord God is an everlasting Rock [the Rock of Ages].
ISAIAH 26:3–4 AMPC

Day 8

Unburdened

Jesus, You're right here beside me—feeling every thrumming nerve ending in my body, the angst in my mind, and the weight of burden pressing on my shoulders. But, Jesus, You promised Your burden was light. So I know this load of stress must not be from You.

The world around me offers nothing but the weight of expectations—expectations I'm woefully unable to consistently meet. The only thing I seem consistent in right now is the failure to live up to a Facebook-perfect life. But then I remember that when I came to You, Jesus, I exchanged all those heavy expectations for free grace. And suddenly, all my failures no longer carry the weight of the world because You are pleased with me. Thank You, Jesus. Amen.

For it is by grace you have been saved, through faith—and this is not from yourselves, it is the gift of God—not by works, so that no one can boast.
EPHESIANS 2:8–9 NIV

Day 9

The Confidence to Be Honest

Dear God, help me find the confidence to be honest with others. Strengthen me with Your strength. Embolden me with Your power. Whether it's sharing my opinion about a situation, giving advice when asked, offering my ideas in a meeting, or just being truthful with a loved one, give me the courage to be candid. I can't do this without You. Bless me with the wisdom to know when to be authentic in loving and kind ways, and let me know when I should be bold and frank. Please give me the discernment to know the difference. I trust You to empower me with the self-assurance I need to navigate these situations every time. In Jesus' name I pray, amen.

The wicked are edgy with guilt, ready to run off even when no one's after them; honest people are relaxed and confident, bold as lions.
PROVERBS 28:1 MSG

Day 10

A Safe Place

Lord, when I am at my wits' end—which happens more than I care to admit—I remember You. For You are my rock and refuge, my place of safety when my entire world feels like it is falling apart. You are the one in whom I can hide until the storm passes or until I have the energy, wisdom, strength, and provision to face the storm I am in.

No matter what happens, even if the earth starts to quake and the mountains start falling into the sea, You will hide me in Your presence, be the hedge of protection I need no matter how big the problem or how strong the wind. For this and so much more, I thank You. Amen.

God is a safe place to hide, ready to help when we need him. We stand fearless at the cliff-edge of doom, courageous in seastorm and earthquake, before the rush and roar of oceans, the tremors that shift mountains. Jacob-wrestling God fights for us, God-of-Angel-Armies protects us. River fountains splash joy, cooling God's city, this sacred haunt of the Most High. God lives here, the streets are safe, God at your service from crack of dawn.
PSALM 46:1–5 MSG

Day 11

When You're Scared to Trust God

Dear God, can I be honest? I'm terrified to trust You. It's not that You've ever let me down—You haven't. It's not that I don't believe in You—I do. But it's so hard for me to let go of control and hand my life over to someone I cannot see with my eyes or touch with my hand. Sometimes it feels like I'm trusting air, and it scares me. Grow my faith. Help me realize Your ways are far superior to mine. And help me remember Your heart for me is always good. From today forward, I want to surrender control and learn to follow Your leading. Help me set aside fear and choose to trust You. In Jesus' name I pray, amen.

Trust in the Lord completely, and do not rely on your own opinions. With all your heart rely on him to guide you, and he will lead you in every decision you make. Become intimate with him in whatever you do, and he will lead you wherever you go.

PROVERBS 3:5–6 TPT

Day 12

An Uplifting Word

Jesus, sometimes negative voices overtake my thoughts. They rail at me in harsh judgment every time I stumble. I hear selfishness, pride, and guilt putting me down, hissing that I am all alone. These murmurs of condemnation *do* feel like a dark cloud hovering over my life. But I know where these voices come from—and it isn't You, Jesus. Because You love me, and Your voice is never harsh, condemning, or demeaning. You are here for me, *always*.

Speak to me, Jesus. Calm my fears. Your grace abounds and stirs the air like a fresh gale. I praise You, Jesus, for saving me. In the absence of condemnation, I can bask in the warm sunshine of Your smile. And I know that You will never leave me. Amen.

With the arrival of Jesus, the Messiah, that fateful dilemma is resolved. Those who enter into Christ's being-here-for-us no longer have to live under a continuous, low-lying black cloud. A new power is in operation. The Spirit of life in Christ, like a strong wind, has magnificently cleared the air, freeing you from a fated lifetime of brutal tyranny at the hands of sin and death.

ROMANS 8:1–2 MSG

Day 13

Keep Working

Dear God, today's verse offers me a great reminder to trust that You'll help me finish the work I've been called to do. Thank You—because I need it! The truth is I usually start out strong in projects and tasks, but my courage often wanes when I come up against problems or criticism. They discourage me and derail my focus. And I find myself scared that I'll mess up or let people down, which effectively keeps me from moving forward. I don't want to live in fear. Instead, I want my faith to be solid, believing You won't leave me to figure everything out on my own. I need You, Father. Without Your help, I'm unable to be strong and courageous. In Jesus' name I pray, amen.

Also David told Solomon his son, Be strong and courageous,
and do it. Fear not, be not dismayed, for the Lord God,
my God, is with you. He will not fail or forsake you until you have
finished all the work for the service of the house of the Lord.
1 Chronicles 28:20 ampc

Day 14

Let Be and Be Still

What I need in this moment is calm, Lord. Help me to get there, to go from panicked to peace-filled. As I rest with You in this moment, my body still and my mouth silent before You, help my fretful thoughts to flow gently out of my mind as I fill that newly emptied space with Your peace and promises. Help me, King of calm, to be as still as the surface of a pond on a windless morning. Help me to let all things be. Help me to know, recognize, and understand that You alone are God of all things, people, and places. You are my Refuge, High Tower, and Stronghold. Together we are one in love, in peace, and in stillness. Amen.

The Lord of hosts is with us; the God of Jacob is our Refuge
(our Fortress and High Tower). Selah [pause, and calmly
think of that]! . . . Let be and be still, and know (recognize
and understand) that I am God. I will be exalted among the
nations! I will be exalted in the earth! The Lord of hosts is
with us; the God of Jacob is our Refuge (our High Tower and
Stronghold). Selah [pause, and calmly think of that]!
PSALM 46:7, 10–11 AMPC

Day 15

Singing over Me

God, over and over Your Word assures me of Your unending love. But my life is full of struggles. And I struggle to believe sometimes that You could possibly be happy with my fumbled attempts at obedience, my constant failures. My heart cries, "Don't look, Jesus, I messed up again!"

Jesus.

Oh, yes, Jesus! The tension inside me eases at Your name; my spirit releases a pent-up breath. Jesus, You did it for me. . .because I couldn't. You lived my righteousness for me, died my death to absorb God's wrath over sin. I am now righteous and blameless! I have been so stressed and worried about never stepping out of line, but You are delighted with me! I'm going to tarry with this truth for a moment: *You. Love. Me.* Father, I see Your smile. Amen.

> *"The LORD your God is with you, the Mighty Warrior who saves. He will take great delight in you; in his love he will no longer rebuke you, but will rejoice over you with singing."*
> ZEPHANIAH 3:17 NIV

Day 16

Remaining Undaunted

Dear God, how am I supposed to be undaunted when my life is full of stress and strife? I look at the state of the world, and it terrifies me. Everyone is bickering, and our nation is divided. I'm struggling in some very important relationships, and it worries me. I'm scared about my financial obligations and lack of income. I'm concerned with my health but too afraid to go talk to a doctor. I'm not sure I could handle a bad diagnosis. My work isn't fulfilling, and I feel hopeless about it. Lord, I need the kind of peace and confidence that comes from You. I am desperate for the fear to take a back seat to my faith. In Jesus' name I pray, amen.

I have told you these things, so that in Me you may have
[perfect] peace and confidence. In the world you have
tribulation and trials and distress and frustration; but be of
good cheer [take courage; be confident, certain, undaunted]!
For I have overcome the world. [I have deprived it of
power to harm you and have conquered it for you.]
JOHN 16:33 AMPC

Day 17

Pleasing God

I want to be so full of faith, to have so much trust in You, Lord, that I please You. But to do that, to be able to approach You, I must believe not just that You exist but that You will respond to me when I come to You with my worries, my woes, and my whys.

So here I am, Lord, standing before You. Fill me with undying faith in You. Remind me that You alone can save me from a life of worries and woes. You alone can help me find my way through this life. And You alone can save me from myself and bring me to the place of peace I crave. In Jesus' name, amen.

By an act of faith, Enoch skipped death completely.
"They looked all over and couldn't find him because God
had taken him." We know on the basis of reliable testimony
that before he was taken "he pleased God." It's impossible to
please God apart from faith. And why? Because anyone who
wants to approach God must believe both that he exists and
that he cares enough to respond to those who seek him.
HEBREWS 11:5–6 MSG

Day 18

The Confidence to Expect God

Dear God, Your Word says that I should expect You to show up in my life. So why do I live in constant fear that You won't be there when I need You? I worry I've sinned too much or angered You one too many times. I feel certain my choices disappoint You on the regular. Sometimes I convince myself that You have bigger issues to deal with and that my asking is nothing more than an inconvenience. I need a shift in perspective so I can live in expectation of You! I want to know without a doubt that Your hands are deep in the frustrations I'm experiencing. And I need God-given confidence that You'll show up. In Jesus' name I pray, amen.

Be brave. Be strong. Don't give up. Expect GOD to get here soon.
PSALM 31:24 MSG

Day 19

Way Maker

God, my stress spikes because I just don't know what to do. Where to turn for help. Which decision is the *right* one. I seek out friends and scavenge between the covers of yet another self-help book—looking for answers, understanding, and wisdom. And then I hear Your voice: "Ask Me."

I've wasted so much anxiety on seeking answers everywhere except the Alpha and Omega, the source of all wisdom. God, what should I do? Please give me wisdom. I will wait patiently for Your answers, because I know You have perfect, unexpected solutions. I doubt the Israelites expected You to make a way through the Red Sea, and yet You did. And You will show me the way through my problems too. Amen.

If any of you lacks wisdom, you should ask God, who gives generously to all without finding fault, and it will be given to you.
JAMES 1:5 NIV

Day 20

Nothing Impossible

Lord, I've been letting worries overtake me, allowing them to crowd out my knowledge of and faith in You. Help me to get back on track. To really focus on who You are and what You've already done in my life.

Revitalize my faith, Lord. Give it life so that I can confidently say to a mountain of an obstacle, "Move from here to there"—and it will move. Help me to live in line with Your will and way so that nothing will be impossible to me. For with that kind of faith in and obedience to You, my worries will wane and my faith fill out as I follow in Your footsteps. Amen.

Then the disciples came to Jesus and asked privately, Why could we not drive it out? He said to them, Because of the littleness of your faith [that is, your lack of firmly relying trust]. For truly I say to you, if you have faith [that is living] like a grain of mustard seed, you can say to this mountain, Move from here to yonder place, and it will move; and nothing will be impossible to you.
MATTHEW 17:19–20 AMPC

Day 21

King of My Heart

God, what things have I placed before You in my heart? I know I have given Your throne away at times. I have told you that *tomorrow* I will read my Bible, *tomorrow* I will pray about the decisions and circumstances that are troubling my sleep, *tomorrow* I will commit to that Bible study or prayer group or even just to reaching out to my neighbor. *Tomorrow.* Because today I have to get things done.

How wrong I have been. You are in all things, and all things are held together by You. And yet, I somehow believe that I can pull together the unraveling threads of my life all by myself. What unmitigated pride I've indulged. God, please forgive me. Help me to crown You King of my heart. Amen.

Dear children, keep away from anything that
might take God's place in your hearts.
1 JOHN 5:21 NLT

Day 22

The Fear of Rejection

Dear God, it's discouraging to hear what others are saying about me. It's like my greatest fears of rejection and judgment are coming true. I actually thought I was liked. I thought I had good friends who loved and cared for me. But it seems I thought I was more liked than I really am. Would You please help me remember I was created on purpose and with a purpose? Whisper into my spirit what makes me lovable in Your eyes. Show me what makes me unique and special. Grow my confidence in who I am because of You and not anything else. And keep me from anchoring my sense of worth in anything the world has to offer. In Jesus' name I pray, amen.

Jesus overheard what they were talking about and said to the leader, "Don't listen to them; just trust me."

MARK 5:36 MSG

Day 23

God Alone

When I hear bad news, Lord, when my future looks more than bleak, help me to keep calm and to come to You for guidance. Remind me who You are and what You have done for Your people since the beginning of time. Lead me to pray for the peace and strength I need to meet every challenge. For You alone are the one who reigns in heaven and on earth. You are infinitely more powerful than any other being. No one—no man, no woman, no king, no queen, no entity—can stand against You. So I come to You for calm and clarity. Speak, Lord. Speak. Amen.

> The armies of the Moabites, Ammonites, and some of the Meunites declared war on Jehoshaphat. . . . Jehoshaphat was terrified. . .and begged the LORD for guidance. He also ordered everyone in Judah to begin fasting. . . . He prayed, "O LORD, God of our ancestors, you alone are the God who is in heaven. You are ruler of all the kingdoms of the earth. You are powerful and mighty; no one can stand against you!"
>
> 2 CHRONICLES 20:1, 3, 6 NLT

Day 24

Talk to Him Always

Lord, You have called me friend, and more. . .beloved daughter. You have established our relationship through Jesus, who made it possible for me—with my dirt-encrusted and ragged edges—to cozy right up to Your throne and say, "Hey, Dad, what do You think about this job opportunity or the problems I'm having with my son? I could use Your advice." After all, what is friendship if not a long conversation between two people—the kind that takes an entire lifetime to close.

And yet, too often in my frazzled life, I drop my end of the dialogue. You want to ease my fears and relieve my burdens. . . I just forget to talk to You about them. Help me to constantly pray. Amen.

Pray constantly, give thanks in everything; for
this is God's will for you in Christ Jesus.
1 Thessalonians 5:17–18 csb

Day 25

The Armor of God

Dear God, thank You for providing heavenly armor that I can access whenever I need it. I'm grateful You created a way to keep me safe and give me confidence. I'm also thankful this armor offers powerful protection against anything that comes my way, be it a scheme in the spirit or a battle here on earth. This armor delivers courage that I will be able to face my fears knowing I'm backed by You. It encourages bravery as I take steps forward in my journey to live a full life. And it reminds me of how much You must love me to make sure I am not left unprotected and unarmed. In Jesus' name I pray, amen.

Put on the full armor of God to protect yourselves from the devil and his evil schemes. We're not waging war against enemies of flesh and blood alone. No, this fight is against tyrants, against authorities, against supernatural powers and demon princes that slither in the darkness of this world, and against wicked spiritual armies that lurk about in heavenly places.
EPHESIANS 6:11–12 VOICE

Day 26

Eyes on God

When trouble is brewing, Lord, and I don't know what to say or think or do, I will come to You. To You I will cry for help. To You I will lift my voice. For I know that You will hear my prayer and attend to my petition. I am confident that against all odds, You will save me.

Lord, I know very well that I have no strength to stand against the trouble brought about by the evil intentions of others, but I also know that nothing can conquer You. I don't know what to do, but my eyes are fixed on You. Amen.

If evil comes upon us. . .we will stand before this house and before You—for Your Name [and the symbol of Your presence] is in this house—and cry to You in our affliction, and You will hear and save. . . . We have no might to stand against this great company that is coming against us. We do not know what to do, but our eyes are upon You.
2 CHRONICLES 20:9, 12 AMPC

Day 27

Every Moment

God, I don't even think about starting my day without a steaming jolt of caffeine. It's automatic. I wake up. I pour coffee. I drink coffee. But have I made You as integral in my day? Do I *need* You like I need caffeine and chocolate? Or have I been doing this life thing on my own, forgetting to acknowledge that I need You every minute of every single day for the rest of my life?

There's no substitute for You. I give You my worries, my stresses, my fears, my insecurities, my spectacular failures, the entire glorious mess—it's Yours. I just need You to sustain me. I trust Your great love for me and Your unmatched power. You will take care of me. Amen.

Cast your cares on the LORD and he will sustain you; he will never let the righteous be shaken. . . . But as for me, I trust in you.

PSALM 55:22–23 NIV

Day 28

Weapons for Victory

Dear God, thank You for knowing that the weapons I need to navigate the ups and downs of this life are not earthly ones. Because my battles are waged in the heavenlies, my arsenal needs to be filled with spiritual armaments. Help me remember my shield of faith is available every time hard seasons hit and fear sets in. I know it will steady me to press into You for wisdom and peace. As I choose to trust Your faithfulness, that invaluable piece of armor will help stop the burning arrows of hate fired right at me. And Your Word, the sword of the Spirit, will teach and instruct me how to live a courageous life of victory rather than defeat. In Jesus' name I pray, amen.

Don't forget to raise the shield of faith above all else,
so you will be able to extinguish flaming spears hurled at
you from the wicked one. Take also the helmet of salvation
and the sword of the Spirit, which is the word of God.
EPHESIANS 6:16–17 VOICE

Day 29

Valley of Blessings

When my worries and troubles are getting me down, Lord, remind me of the way You handled the armies against Your people. How You fought for people and how their praises to You ended up being their most powerful weapon against their foes. And not only did You bring them an amazing victory but You gifted them with so much spoil it took them three days to gather it all up! You are more than a wonder-worker, more than a refuge and stronghold. You are the Lord of miracles and the God of blessings to whom I lift my voice in praise. Amen.

When they began to sing and to praise, the Lord set
ambushments against the men of Ammon, Moab, and
Mount Seir. . . . They all helped to destroy one another. . . .
Jehoshaphat and his people. . .were three days in gathering
the spoil. On the fourth day they assembled in the Valley
of Beracah. There they blessed the Lord. So the name of
the place is still called the Valley of Beracah [blessing].
2 CHRONICLES 20:22–23, 25–26 AMPC

Day 30

Above All Else

God, why do I allow worry to choke out my peace and joy—my sense of security? I'm striving after things that You've told me I don't need to worry over. Help me to seek You *first*—and seek You *always*. You are intimately acquainted with all my needs. You understand my fears and know my desires.

Lord, my stress stems from not seeking Your kingdom above all else. Show me the things that I have been running after, Father, that are not of Your kingdom. I want to walk away from sin, not because I think I can earn Your love, but because You already love me. And I love You. Teach me to rest as serenely in Your care as the luxuriously gowned wildflowers. Amen.

"If God cares so wonderfully for wildflowers that are here today and thrown into the fire tomorrow, he will certainly care for you. Why do you have so little faith? So don't worry about these things, saying, 'What will we eat? What will we drink? What will we wear?' These things dominate the thoughts of unbelievers, but your heavenly Father already knows all your needs. Seek the Kingdom of God above all else, and live righteously, and he will give you everything you need."

MATTHEW 6:30–33 NLT

Day 31

Empowered Prayer

Dear God, Your Word says to pray at all times and with all kinds of prayers. It doesn't mince words when it also says to ask for everything I need. This seems like an expectation rather than a suggestion. And honestly, it feels like You're inviting me to talk to You all day long about anything and everything. Whether I am worried or afraid, You want to hear from me. When I feel hopeless, I should pray. When I need Your comfort or guidance, I can talk to You about it. My days would be better if I lived this verse because the enemy wouldn't have any space to stir me up and whisper terrifying thoughts into my heart. Thank You! In Jesus' name I pray, amen.

Pray at all times (on every occasion, in every season) in the Spirit, with all [manner of] prayer and entreaty. To that end keep alert and watch with strong purpose and perseverance, interceding in behalf of all the saints (God's consecrated people).
EPHESIANS 6:18 AMPC

Day 32

By Faith

Lord, I can imagine all the ribbing Noah got as he followed Your command to build an enormous boat and, to complicate matters, did so "in the middle of dry land"! All because You warned him of what was coming, something he could not yet see or hear. He acted only on what You told him. And because of his faith in You and his willingness to obey no matter how much he was mocked, he not only was able to save his family—as well as the future of humankind and animal-kind—but became even closer to You! So many blessings rolled into one act of extreme faith in extreme times. Help me to be a Noah, Lord—to follow You and Your commands no matter how it looks in the eyes of an unbelieving world. In Jesus' name, amen.

By faith, Noah built a ship in the middle of dry land. He was warned about something he couldn't see, and acted on what he was told. The result? His family was saved. His act of faith drew a sharp line between the evil of the unbelieving world and the rightness of the believing world. As a result, Noah became intimate with God.
HEBREWS 11:7 MSG

Day 33

Greener Pastures

Jesus, my strong, sure shepherd, You have made things so good for me! But this world and our enemy are so accomplished at making sin look delectable. I might even convince myself that it's better than what You've given me. . .but then I remember that the wages of sin is death. And You've given me wonderful life!

Here in Your soft green grass I rest from my stress. I put my hope and trust in Your capable hands. When I take in the place You've led me to—undeserved grace, love that You will never take back, and righteousness as if I'd never been stained by sin—how could I ever wish to walk out of this meadow? Father, may I never again think the grass is greener outside Your pastures. Amen.

GOD, my shepherd! I don't need a thing. You have bedded me down in lush meadows, you find me quiet pools to drink from. True to your word, you let me catch my breath and send me in the right direction. Even when the way goes through Death Valley, I'm not afraid when you walk at my side. Your trusty shepherd's crook makes me feel secure.

PSALM 23:1–4 MSG

Day 34

Victory against Fear and Shame

Dear God, I struggle with guilt and shame. I have messed up so much, making bad choices more than I care to share. Not only does it feel like what I've done is wrong, but it feels like who I am is wrong. And it's because of those painful feelings that I've hidden from You. But Your Word says that if I ask, You will give me the ability to stand up to the temptation and make the right choice. What's more, You say every test I face is an opportunity to grow my faith in You as I choose to trust Your helping hand. I don't have to be afraid anymore! I can stand in victory because You've made a way. In Jesus' name I pray, amen.

We all experience times of testing, which is normal for every human being. But God will be faithful to you. He will screen and filter the severity, nature, and timing of every test or trial you face so that you can bear it. And each test is an opportunity to trust him more, for along with every trial God has provided for you a way of escape that will bring you out of it victoriously.
1 CORINTHIANS 10:13 TPT

Day 35

The Desire to Be Optimistic

Dear God, Your Word clearly says not to be dismayed. It instructs us not to be discouraged or downcast in the battles we face every day. But that's a tall order. How am I supposed to be optimistic when I'm watching important relationships crumble? How can I be hopeful when the doctors aren't optimistic in the treatment plan? How can I be expectant when I look at the state of the world? And Lord, how can I be positive when my finances are failing? I am desperate for peace and joy. I'm tired of feeling negative. I want hope and happiness instead of dismay. Please let these reign in my heart as I place my faith in Your hands. In Jesus' name I pray, amen.

Then you will prosper if you are careful to keep and fulfill the statutes and ordinances with which the Lord charged Moses concerning Israel. Be strong and of good courage. Dread not and fear not; be not dismayed.

1 CHRONICLES 22:13 AMPC

Day 36

In Step with God

In step with You, Lord, I know I need not fear or dread anything. Because You are with me. You use Your rod to protect me and Your staff to guide me. I need no other reassurance than that, for You are my Comforter. With You on my side, my enemies are powerless to hurt me or steal my peace. You have anointed me with Your Spirit, and I know that only goodness, mercy, and love will follow me all my life as I dwell in You. Amen.

Yes, though I walk through the [deep, sunless] valley of the shadow of death, I will fear or dread no evil, for You are with me; Your rod [to protect] and Your staff [to guide], they comfort me. You prepare a table before me in the presence of my enemies. You anoint my head with oil; my [brimming] cup runs over. Surely or only goodness, mercy, and unfailing love shall follow me all the days of my life, and through the length of my days the house of the Lord [and His presence] shall be my dwelling place.

PSALM 23:4–6 AMPC

Day 37

All-Powerful

Lord, I'm afraid to let go and give You control. But this mindset leaves me with nothing but anxiety. I feel small and fearful when I admit I can't control much of anything. But You, Lord, are the master of all. You have all the power. A mere word from You snapped a universe into existence and breathed life into dead matter.

Father, bolster my trust in You—in Your power over this world; in Your great, unmatched love for me; in Your wisdom to work all things out for good for those who love You and are called according to Your purpose. In relinquishing control to You, I find rest from my constant striving because I believe—I *know*—that You can handle the circumstances causing my stress. Amen.

"He spreads out the northern skies over empty space; he suspends the earth over nothing. . . . The pillars of the heavens quake, aghast at his rebuke. By his power he churned up the sea. . . . And these are but the outer fringe of his works; how faint the whisper we hear of him! Who then can understand the thunder of his power?"

JOB 26:7, 11–12, 14 NIV

Day 38

Unafraid

Dear God, help me remember that You are the one who saves me. It's not food or alcohol. It's not people or a full calendar. It's not a trendy spiritual awakening or meditation. It's not medication or a new wardrobe. Nothing in the world can save me from my fears and insecurities like You can. Everything else offers short-term relief to a long-term battle. It's because of You, because my trust is firmly planted in Your love, that I can live unafraid. I can be confident in scary times, knowing You promise to be with me always. I can hope because You won't leave me trapped and alone. I receive Your love! In Jesus' name I pray, amen.

"Behold—God is my salvation! I am confident, unafraid, and I will trust in you." Yes! The Lord Yah is my might and my melody; he has become my salvation!

ISAIAH 12:2 TPT

Day 39

The Extra Mile

Some things that I might worry about, Lord, are things You want me to allow to happen. If someone hurts me, I'm to remain vulnerable and allow her to injure me again. If anyone takes my shirt, I'm to give him my coat. If someone forces me to walk one mile with her, I'm to go an extra mile as well. And I'm to give to the one who begs, while allowing another to borrow. All of those things seem to go against what might give me peace. Yet that's how You work, wanting us to live by our spirit, not by our flesh. If that's what You want, I'm up for living that way, Lord, as long as You stay by my side. For with You beside me on this journey, I know all will be well. Amen.

"If anyone slaps you on the right cheek, turn to him the other also. And if anyone would sue you and take your tunic, let him have your cloak as well. And if anyone forces you to go one mile, go with him two miles. Give to the one who begs from you, and do not refuse the one who would borrow from you."

Matthew 5:39–42 esv

Day 40

A New Game Plan

God, I trust You. I know that You are able and that You love me. But I harbor fears that lead to stress. Fears about my finances, my children's future, my health. At times this world can feel like such an uncertain and dangerous place. And evil things do happen. . .so I need to put in play a game plan to win victory over my stress.

Father, I will meditate on Your Word so that Your truth and promises overtake my thoughts and crowd out the enemy's lies. Lord, help me see the unhealthy ways that I try to handle my stress, like binge eating or snapping at my family, so I can turn toward You as my ultimate stress reliever. In Jesus' name, amen.

Don't be gullible in regard to smooth-talking evil.
Stay alert like this, and before you know it the God
of peace will come down on Satan with both feet,
stomping him into the dirt. Enjoy the best of Jesus!
ROMANS 16:20 MSG

Day 41

The World's Peace Is Fragile

Dear God, I could use a big dose of peace in my life. These days, peace feels terribly elusive. With my crazy life, I am stirred up most of the time. My emotions swirl around me as I try to calm my anxious heart. How do I stop my mind from spinning? How do I find rest when I can't slow my thoughts down? You offer Your peace to those who ask, knowing it will bring a confident stillness that will lead to courage. Too often I look to the world for a remedy, but it only offers a fragile kind of peace that breaks with too much expectation. Lord, please bring Your peace into my life. In Jesus' name I pray, amen.

"I leave the gift of peace with you—my peace. Not the kind of fragile peace given by the world, but my perfect peace. Don't yield to fear or be troubled in your hearts—instead, be courageous!"

JOHN 14:27 TPT

Day 42

By an Act of Faith

I can't imagine packing up my family and household goods, leaving my home, and going on a trip to a place I've never seen before. Heading out without a map, just waiting for You to say, "Stop here. This is the place." Yet that's what You called Abraham to do. And that's what You call me to do. To go where no woman has gone before, walking Your way, according to Your promise and timeline. That takes a leap of faith. Yet I know You are a God who keeps His Word. So here I am, Lord. Tell me where You would have me go. And as I follow in faith, give me peace for the journey. In Jesus' name, amen.

By an act of faith, Abraham said yes to God's call to travel to an unknown place that would become his home. When he left he had no idea where he was going. By an act of faith he lived in the country promised him, lived as a stranger camping in tents. Isaac and Jacob did the same, living under the same promise.

HEBREWS 11:8–9 MSG

Day 43

Peace Is Yours

Lord, I need Your peace to descend upon the troubled waters of my mind. When the winds kick up and the waters become choppy, my stress rises. When my heart is troubled, I need Your peace to cocoon my troubled mind in peace—the peace that passes all understanding. Because You, Jesus, can stand in the midst of my storm and say, "Be still!"

Lord, even if the storm is still raging around me, my soul is at peace. Send Your peace to guard my heart and mind today against the fears that assault me. Jesus, when I put my trust in Your power over the storms, my fears shrink and I am no longer afraid. Help me to remember that Your peace is already mine. Amen.

Peace I leave with you; my peace I give you. I do not give to you as the world gives. Do not let your hearts be troubled and do not be afraid.

John 14:27 niv

Day 44

With God by Your Side

Dear God, Your Word says that with You by my side I can be free of fear, unafraid of anything that comes my way. It says to lay all my fears out before You and stand in unmovable trust because You will give me the help I need to overcome them. I want to believe it's as simple as that, but I know what's often easy to say is difficult to walk out. Please give me the strength to make decisions that set me up for freedom. Grow my faith so I trust in You with all my heart. I don't want anything to keep me from the peace You promise. And I want to experience it every single day. In Jesus' name I pray, amen.

But in the day that I'm afraid, I lay all my fears before you and trust in you with all my heart. What harm could a man bring to me? With God on my side, I will not be afraid of what comes. The roaring praises of God fill my heart as I trust his promises.

PSALM 56:3–4 TPT

Day 45

Under His Wings

Lead me into Your presence, Lord. Help me find rest in Your shadow. For You alone are my refuge. You are my fortress, a place where no one can touch me. You, my Lord and Savior, are my God—*the* God. In You alone I trust. For I know You will rescue me from every trap that is set against me. You will protect me from any harm headed my way. Best of all, You, like a father eagle, will cover me with Your feathers, providing me shelter, whether good weather or foul. You have surrounded me with Your presence, Your promises, and Your protection—all of which birth peace within me. Amen.

Those who live in the shelter of the Most High will find rest in the shadow of the Almighty. This I declare about the LORD: He alone is my refuge, my place of safety; he is my God, and I trust him. For he will rescue you from every trap and protect you from deadly disease. He will cover you with his feathers. He will shelter you with his wings. His faithful promises are your armor and protection.

PSALM 91:1–4 NLT

Day 46

A New Way of Thinking

Lord, I don't want to be stuck in my old pattern of thinking, doing things the same worn-out way and getting the same tired, disappointing results. Change my way of thinking and bring it into the light of Your good and holy ways.

The world says I should fear for my future and stress about things that are beyond my control, but You say that I can pray. That You will hear my prayer and answer me. And that You will never leave me or forsake me. I'm suddenly seeing my stress-inducing fears in a whole new way. I know that *nothing* is beyond Your control. And I *fully* trust You, because You love me and have good plans for my future. Amen.

Do not conform to the pattern of this world, but be transformed by the renewing of your mind. Then you will be able to test and approve what God's will is—his good, pleasing and perfect will.

ROMANS 12:2 NIV

Day 47

God's Answers

Dear God, I need the kind of faith that doesn't waver based on Your responses to my prayers. I need to be steadfast in my faith, unshakable in my reliance on You. In my heart, I know You're capable of saving me from my fears and insecurities. I completely believe there is nothing You cannot accomplish. And I trust You will do what is best for me as well as what glorifies Your holy name. You are a good Father! But if You choose to answer my prayers differently than I'd hoped, let me remember You are still worthy of my devotion. You are still a faithful God. And I can still ask You for what I need. In Jesus' name I pray, amen.

*If you throw us into the blazing furnace, then the God we serve
is able to rescue us from a furnace of blazing fire and release
us from your power, Your Majesty. But even if He does not,
O king, you can be sure that we still will not serve your gods
and we will not worship the golden statue you erected.*
DANIEL 3:17–18 VOICE

Day 48

A Win-Win Situation

So many benefits come with making You my refuge, Lord. When I depend on You and trust in You, I always end up in a win-win situation. When I trust You to be my refuge, when I have the sense and faith to dwell in You, You—the one powerful God of the universe—not only promise that no harm will come to me but also promise to order Your angels to watch over me, to protect me in every way. You have commanded them to support me with their hands so I don't trip up.

For all this and so much more, Lord, I thank You—with all my heart, all my thanks, and all my praise. Amen.

Because you have made the LORD—my refuge, the Most High—your dwelling place, no harm will come to you; no plague will come near your tent. For He will give His angels orders concerning you, to protect you in all your ways. They will support you with their hands so that you will not strike your foot against a stone.

PSALM 91:9–12 HCSB

Day 49

Faith under Pressure

Father, usually when I find myself in the midst of difficult situations, my prayer is "Get me out of here!" I ask You to take away the hard times because I want relief from the stress and pressure. But You've shown me a different perspective on these hard times. They're a gift—a gift that is working to transform me into a person who is more like You, Jesus. And Your life is the ultimate model.

These stress-inducing times are refining my faith, contouring me into someone who is more loving, more compassionate, more patient, more kind—more like You, Jesus. Now instead of running from the hard stuff, I thank You for the work it's doing to change and strengthen me. Amen.

Consider it a sheer gift, friends, when tests and challenges come at you from all sides. You know that under pressure, your faith-life is forced into the open and shows its true colors. So don't try to get out of anything prematurely. Let it do its work so you become mature and well-developed, not deficient in any way.

JAMES 1:2–4 MSG

Day 50

Brave No Matter What

Dear God, would You please strengthen me! I don't want to be the kind of woman who lives in defeat, afraid of anything and everything that comes my way. Instead, I want to thrive in the victory that only comes from nurturing a trusting faith in You, confident I will receive all I need to stand strong and face the inevitable and difficult storms of life. Help me find courage as I choose You over anything the world offers. My heart's desire is to be fearless, knowing I can do all things through Christ, who gives me strength. I don't want to trust small. I want to believe big! Help me be brave, no matter what. In Jesus' name I pray, amen.

If you faint in the day of adversity, your strength is small.
PROVERBS 24:10 AMPC

Day 51

A Personal Knowledge of God

I want to know more about You, Lord. For the more I know about You, the fewer my worries and the greater my peace of mind, the fewer my frets and the greater my faith. Lead me, Lord, through Your Word. Tell me what You would have me know. Show me where You would have me go. Reveal what You would have me see. Say what You would have me hear. For as I learn more about Your faithfulness to me, I'll understand that You will never leave me. That when I call, You will answer. That when I'm in trouble, You'll deliver me. Amen.

Because he has set his love upon Me, therefore will I deliver
him; I will set him on high, because he knows and understands
My name [has a personal knowledge of My mercy, love, and
kindness—trusts and relies on Me, knowing I will never forsake
him, no, never]. He shall call upon Me, and I will answer him;
I will be with him in trouble, I will deliver him and honor him.
With long life will I satisfy him and show him My salvation.

PSALM 91:14–16 AMPC

Day 52

Hard-Pressed Prayers

Lord, I'm feeling the crushing force of hard places. I'm anxious and afraid. I look all around for a way out, for answers. . .but I don't cry out to You. I forget to pray about my problems.

Lord, the Psalms say that when I feel hard pressed, when it seems like circumstances box me in and fear scratches at me, I can cry out to You—and You will bring me into an open place. You will give me breathing space. You promise that You are with me and will never leave me. I release my fears to You, the way maker. When I'm ready to give up, You show up with solutions I never could have imagined—I only have to ask. Thank You, Jesus. Amen.

When hard pressed, I cried to the LORD; he brought me into a spacious place. The LORD is with me; I will not be afraid. What can mere mortals do to me?

PSALM 118:5–6 NIV

Day 53

Reinforced Resolve

Dear God, help me remember that ultimately, You're my defender. I know there are times You require me to advocate for myself and stand up to my fears, but there are other times when You're the one to conquer what opposes me. Either way, I'm so thankful knowing You promise to be with me. I'll be honest, though—sometimes it feels too overwhelming to face my fears even though I know You are present. I worry about what others might think if I stand my ground. So, God, in those times, let me feel Your fatherly protection boosting my bravery. Reinforce my resolve. And give me grit and guts to be strong, knowing You have my back. In Jesus' name I pray, amen.

Yahweh is my revelation-light and the source of my salvation. I fear no one! I'll never turn back and run, for you, Yahweh, surround and protect me. When evil ones come to destroy me, they will be the ones who turn back.

Psalm 27:1–2 TPT

Day 54

Surrendering Worries

Dear God, I'm feeling hopeless. I'm worried certain things in my life won't change, and it scares me. Your Word says Jesus came for freedom, but I feel stuck. It says You will fill me to overflowing with joy and peace that cannot be contained, but I am disheartened instead. I'm desperate for You to fill my heart with encouragement that everything will be okay. Would You graciously change my attitude so I can expect Your good works? Let the Holy Spirit replace my overwhelming fears with overwhelming faith. And I would deeply appreciate a shift in perspective so I can surrender my worries as I wait for You to fill me with hopefulness and inspiration for the future! In Jesus' name I pray, amen.

Now may God, the fountain of hope, fill you to overflowing
with uncontainable joy and perfect peace as you trust in him.
And may the power of the Holy Spirit continually surround your
life with his super-abundance until you radiate with hope!
ROMANS 15:13 TPT

Day 55

The Water Walker

Lord of all, when I am surrounded by clouds and darkness, when I find myself in panic mode, help me recognize the comfort and deliverance that come with Your presence. Help me not to react in fear. When You are looking to be there for me, to be my guard and rescuer, open up my ears and my mind to Your words: "Do not be afraid. I am here."

For when I realize who You are, I will be eager to let You into my boat. For I know that when You, the great I Am, are sailing with me, I will reach my true destination more swiftly. In Your name I pray, amen.

> *[Jesus' disciples] got into the boat and headed across the lake toward Capernaum. Soon a gale swept down upon them, and the sea grew very rough. They had rowed three or four miles when suddenly they saw Jesus walking on the water toward the boat. They were terrified, but he called out to them, "Don't be afraid. I am here!" Then they were eager to let him in the boat, and immediately they arrived at their destination!*
>
> JOHN 6:17–21 NLT

Day 56

Whom Shall I Fear?

Lord, You are the God of the universe. It's easy to skip right on by the magnitude of that fact. So I want to sit with this knowledge for a moment and meditate on just who You are.

Astrophysicists say that the universe contains more than 100 billion galaxies. 100 *billion*—with a *B*. And probably more. One hundred billion galaxies and counting. . . That's unfathomable. The depths of Your knowledge and power are every bit as unfathomable, God. And yet I stress over the economy or my kids' attitudes.

The God of 100 billion galaxies knows my name, cares about my problems, and promises never to leave me or forsake me. Now *that's* unfathomable! Father, forgive me for losing sight of just who is fighting for me. Amen.

In my distress I prayed to the LORD, and the LORD answered me and set me free. The LORD is for me, so I will have no fear. What can mere people do to me?
PSALM 118:5–6 NLT

Day 57

The Weight of Guilt

Dear God, I feel a million fingers pointing at me all the time. Every day I wake up with a sense of guilt, and I can't pinpoint it. I worry that I'm doing something wrong, always expecting to hear a judgmental comment. Why is guilt so oppressive in my life? I know Jesus came to the world and died to remove my sin—and that includes any guilt from my sin. But I cannot seem to shake the guilt. In Your kindness, would You supernaturally lift this from me? If there's something I need to change, I'm listening. But if not, hear my plea to remove this unnecessary guilt. It's too heavy for my heart to carry another day. In Jesus' name I pray, amen.

Who will bring a charge against God's elect people? It is God who acquits them. Who is going to convict them? It is Christ Jesus who died, even more, who was raised, and who also is at God's right side. It is Christ Jesus who also pleads our case for us.
ROMANS 8:33–34 CEB

Day 58

Nothing Too Difficult

Sometimes, Lord, when I'm in a difficult situation and see no way out, remind me who You are—the one who made the heavens and the earth by Your power and strength. Nothing is too difficult for You. There is no stone You cannot lift, no sea You cannot divide, no wind You cannot tame, no desert You cannot reclaim, no force You cannot defeat. You are the almighty God. At the same time, You are my gentle shepherd, the one who loves me like no other. With You, the greatest, mightiest, and most loving God, by my side and within my heart, I know I never need to be afraid. Amen.

"Ah, Lord GOD! It is you who have made the heavens and the earth by your great power and by your outstretched arm! Nothing is too hard for you. You show steadfast love to thousands, but you repay the guilt of fathers to their children after them, O great and mighty God, whose name is the LORD of hosts, great in counsel and mighty in deed."

JEREMIAH 32:17–19 ESV

Day 59

Guard Your Mind

God, I realize that this life is an epic battle between good and evil: the battle for my mind. My enemy knows that if he can gain control of my mind, then he has won; because when my sinful nature controls my mind, it leads only to death. But when my thoughts are under the guidance of Your Spirit, I have peace and life.

Lord, help me to heed the Spirit's whispers and reject my own self-seeking thoughts. Your Spirit urges me to live God's way—to walk in faith and peace, not be paralyzed by worry and fear. Lord, help me to recognize when anxious thoughts are battling for victory in my mind. I need to take notice of what is causing my stress and call out the lies of the enemy that feed my anxiety. Amen.

The mind governed by the flesh is death, but the mind governed by the Spirit is life and peace.

ROMANS 8:6 NIV

Day 60

The Fear of Separation

Dear God, sometimes I'm afraid that my past choices or current season of sinning will cause You to walk away from me in frustration. I worry there is something in my life that will inevitably separate us. I know Your Word is clear when it says there's nothing and no one that can cause that to happen. But honestly, I struggle to believe it because I've done some horrible things—things I've not told anyone. I don't want to waste my life living in the fear that I may cause You to walk away. So would You speak deep into my heart the truth that You will never leave me? Would You settle that in my heart? In Jesus' name I pray, amen.

Who shall ever separate us from Christ's love? Shall suffering and affliction and tribulation? Or calamity and distress? Or persecution or hunger or destitution or peril or sword?
ROMANS 8:35 AMPC

Day 61

Beloved Shepherd

In Your presence, Lord, I close my eyes and feel Your love surrounding me. I can feel Your left hand cradling my head, Your right hand pulling me close. I can feel Your breath upon my skin, hear Your heartbeat in rhythm with mine. Where You are is where I want to be, my beloved. For You are my gentle shepherd, the one who hears when I cry, the one who stays by my side until my fears have waned. And when You say, "Rise up, My love, My fair one, and come away," You know I will follow You willingly, wherever You would have me go. For You are my beloved shepherd. Amen.

His banner over me was love [for love waved as a protecting and comforting banner over my head when I was near him]. . . . [I can feel] his left hand under my head and his right hand embraces me! . . . [Vividly she pictured it] The voice of my beloved [shepherd]! Behold, he comes, leaping upon the mountains. . . . My beloved speaks and says to me, Rise up, my love, my fair one, and come away.
SONG OF SOLOMON 2:4, 6, 8, 10 AMPC

Day 62

Rest in His Strength

Lord, I've tried doing things all by myself. I've trusted in my own plans and put my faith in my own initiative. Pride has convinced me that I've accomplished my goals with no one to thank but myself.

Father, please forgive my lack of trust in You and my arrogance for believing that I am the great mover and shaker. Because when I put my faith and trust in myself, when things go wrong or I'm staring a situation that I have zero control over in the face, I have nowhere to turn. Teach me to rely on You. Teach me to wait for You. I have definitely made a mess of things in the past because I was impatient. Lord, my hope is in Your faithful love. Amen.

He is not impressed by the strength of a horse; he does not value the power of a warrior. The LORD values those who fear him, those who put their hope in his faithful love.
PSALM 147:10–11 CSB

Day 63

A Continual Conversation

Dear God, thank You for reminding me that asking for Your help isn't a once-and-done proposition. Instead, it's an ongoing conversation. It's a continual request. And when I purpose to connect with You daily to grow our personal relationship, it keeps me connected with my source for everything. When I need courage to face my fears, You give it. When I need strength to try again, I get it directly from You. When I need peace and comfort, You provide it. When I'm lacking wisdom or discernment, You are the one who brings it in spades. Every day, give me confidence to pursue our relationship that I may receive the gifts that come from choosing to walk with You. In Jesus' name I pray, amen.

Pursue the LORD and his strength; seek his face always!
1 CHRONICLES 16:11 CEB

Day 64

Source of Comfort

When I am weary, fearful, upset, grieving, or worried, I look for You, Lord. For You alone can see into my heart and mind and know what I need and long for. For You are the Father of all mercy and the God of all comfort. When I am troubled, I need look no further than You, seeking Your calm, Your peace, Your encouragement, Your understanding and comfort. Remind me, Lord, that at some point, when my time of difficulty is over, I will be equipped to encourage, to comfort, to listen to others suffering from the same troubles I've already endured. In Jesus' name.

Blessed be the God and Father of our Lord Jesus Christ, the Father of sympathy (pity and mercy) and the God [Who is the Source] of every comfort (consolation and encouragement), Who comforts (consoles and encourages) us in every trouble (calamity and affliction), so that we may also be able to comfort (console and encourage) those who are in any kind of trouble or distress, with the comfort (consolation and encouragement) with which we ourselves are comforted (consoled and encouraged) by God.
2 Corinthians 1:3–4 ampc

Day 65

Bringing Down Giants

Lord, Goliaths still plunder the lands You have given us. I combat the giants of fear, stress, and anxiety with alarming frequency. They scoff at me just as Goliath jeered at David for coming into the fight with five smooth stones.

But praise You, God! For You are still in the business of bringing down mammoth enemies in the face of overwhelming odds. David taught me that when I come against big problems in this world, I can face them bravely and say in faith, "I come against you in the name of the Lord Almighty!" You have promised to fight for me. I am not wading in alone. May others see my faith in You and Your care for me and recognize that there is a mighty God in heaven. Amen.

David said to the Philistine, "You come against me with sword and spear and javelin, but I come against you in the name of the Lord Almighty, the God of the armies of Israel, whom you have defied. This day the Lord will deliver you into my hands, and I'll strike you down and cut off your head. This very day I will give the carcasses of the Philistine army to the birds and the wild animals, and the whole world will know that there is a God in Israel."

1 Samuel 17:45–46 niv

Day 66

Community

Dear God, I crave to be in community with people. I want friends to spend time with and to walk through life together. But I'm terrified to put myself out there again because it's not gone well in the past. I've been betrayed and left out, judged and criticized, and it's kept me isolated. What if the same thing happens again? Help me find grace to release those who've hurt me and courage to try one more time. You didn't create us to be alone. Your intention has always been for us to be united in one spirit and mind. And Your hope is for me to find a community of people and thrive! Please help me. In Jesus' name I pray, amen.

Most important, live together in a manner worthy of Christ's gospel. Do this, whether I come and see you or I'm absent and hear about you. Do this so that you stand firm, united in one spirit and mind as you struggle together to remain faithful to the gospel.
PHILIPPIANS 1:27 CEB

Day 67

Prompted by Faith

Lord, I'm amazed at some of the choices Your people made under the worst of circumstances. I envy the faith they had in You. Today, I claim that measure of faith for myself.

Today, I refuse to be frightened by the evil behavior of others, people who don't know You. No matter what statements they make or actions they take, I'm counting on You to keep me safe and sound. Then, in that calm place, I know my faith will lead me where You want me to go. And no matter how arduous the journey, all that will matter is that I'm taking it with You. Amen.

[Prompted] by faith Moses, after his birth, was kept concealed for three months by his parents, because they saw how comely the child was; and they were not overawed and terrified by the king's decree. [Aroused] by faith Moses, when he had grown to maturity and become great, refused to be called the son of Pharaoh's daughter, because he preferred to share the oppression [suffer the hardships] and bear the shame of the people of God rather than to have the fleeting enjoyment of a sinful life.
HEBREWS 11:23–25 AMPC

Day 68

Power through Weakness

Lord, I'm so relieved that I don't have to be strong for You. My weakness does not deter You. I don't have to "get it all together" to be used by You. In fact, my pride in my abilities is a stumbling block to Your power.

You lift up the humble who recognize their need for You. When I become smaller and weaker, then Christ in me becomes stronger and His power flows into my life. Otherwise, I might be tempted to take credit for things that You have done, Jesus.

I no longer want to complain about my weaknesses or see them as punishments from an angry God. Help me to rejoice in my weaknesses as Paul did, so I may live more powerfully through You. Amen.

"My grace is all you need. My power works best in weakness."
So now I am glad to boast about my weaknesses, so that the power
of Christ can work through me. That's why I take pleasure in my
weaknesses, and in the insults, hardships, persecutions, and troubles
that I suffer for Christ. For when I am weak, then I am strong.
2 CORINTHIANS 12:9–10 NLT

Day 69

A Divine Boost in Confidence

Dear God, would You give me the courage to be an advocating voice in my community? I want to make a difference, but it scares me to be bold. I worry what others might think. I'm nervous that I'll say the wrong thing. I'm anxious others won't care what I have to say. It's just nerve-racking. But Lord, I feel You calling me out of my comfort zone into new territory, and I'll need a divine boost in confidence. I care about my community and am passionate to help where I can. Thank You for putting this desire in my heart. Now I'm trusting You to open the right doors and to make me brave to do Your work! In Jesus' name I pray, amen.

Be strong, and let us fight bravely for the sake of
our people and the cities of our True God, and may
the Eternal do what seems good in His sight.
2 SAMUEL 10:12 VOICE

Day 70

Motivated by Faith

Make me more like Moses, Lord. Although he had times when he lacked confidence in himself, he never lacked confidence in You. That's how he was able to stay on the right pathway, not allowing anyone—no matter how powerful or evil—to keep him from doing what You called him to do.

Even though I can't see You with my physical eyes, I have faith in Your presence, power, and purpose. For I seek Your Spirit within me, knowing that with You in my heart, mind, and soul, I can do anything You call me to do. You alone are my motivation to live this life for You. In Jesus' name, amen.

[Motivated] by faith he left Egypt behind him, being unawed and undismayed by the wrath of the king; for he never flinched but held staunchly to his purpose and endured steadfastly as one who gazed on Him Who is invisible. By faith (simple trust and confidence in God) he instituted and carried out the Passover and the sprinkling of the blood [on the doorposts], so that the destroyer of the firstborn (the angel) might not touch those [of the children of Israel].
HEBREWS 11:27–28 AMPC

Day 71

My Provision

Lord, Your goodness flows freely through the floodgates of Your abundance to those who look for and depend on You. Yet I can be so hardheaded in my belief that I am self-made. I emphasize the *I* in "I can do all things" and completely neglect the one who does the impossible on my behalf.

Lord, don't ever let me forget the second half of this verse: "through Christ who strengthens me." Oh Father, how my stress rises when I forget that I need Your strength to sustain me. Teach me to wait quietly for You, Lord, instead of pushing and forcing my own agenda. You are my provision—everything I'll ever need. In the name of Jesus, amen.

The Lord is good to those who depend on him, to those who search for him. So it is good to wait quietly for salvation from the Lord.
LAMENTATIONS 3:25–26 NLT

Day 72

Producing a Fearlessness

Dear God, I know the last thing I need to do when I'm afraid is run and hide. Even when everything in me wants to pull the covers over my head and disappear, Your encouragement is always to trust in Your will and ways. Your Word says You use all things for my good. You use troubled times to grow my faith, increase my endurance, refine my character, and instill hope. If I try to avoid any rough seasons, I risk missing out on the gifts that come from them. I must choose faith over fear, and I will need Your help. Produce a fearlessness in me that's made possible through trusting You in every situation. In Jesus' name I pray, amen.

But that's not all! Even in times of trouble we have a joyful confidence, knowing that our pressures will develop in us patient endurance. And patient endurance will refine our character, and proven character leads us back to hope. And this hope is not a disappointing fantasy, because we can now experience the endless love of God cascading into our hearts through the Holy Spirit who lives in us!
ROMANS 5:3–5 TPT

Day 73

An Outstretched Arm

Amazingly enough, Lord, *nothing* is too difficult for You. That fact is proven by Your Word, which holds numerous examples of You doing what seems impossible. You made the sun stand still for Joshua. You turned five fish and two loaves of bread into enough food to feed five thousand men—not including the women and children with them! You whisked Elijah away on a fiery chariot that carried him up to heaven. You parted the sea, walked on water, and calmed the waves. If You can do all that and so much more, I know You can lead me to a place of peace. In Your name, amen.

You brought forth Your people Israel out of the land of Egypt with signs and wonders, with a strong hand and outstretched arm. . .You gave them this land which You swore to their fathers to give them, a land flowing with milk and honey; and they entered and took possession of it. . . . Then came the word of the Lord to Jeremiah, saying, Behold, I am the Lord, the God of all flesh; is there anything too hard for Me?
JEREMIAH 32:21–23, 26–27 AMPC

Day 74

Work in Progress

Heavenly Father, I am beyond overjoyed that You don't give up on me! You've promised that I'm a work in progress until the day Jesus comes back. I can let go of my fears that my mess-ups might be too much for You. I am not too much for You, Father. My mess is not too big, and my problems are not too complicated for You.

Please soften the dried clay of my heart so that it yields to Your sculpting hand. Strengthen me to heed Your Holy Spirit's urgings. You are the master artist who would mold my heart into a thing of beauty when I surrender my will to Yours. Even when I falter, You're capable of redeeming my past and making me more like Jesus. Amen.

And I am certain that God, who began the good work within you, will continue his work until it is finally finished on the day when Christ Jesus returns.
PHILIPPIANS 1:6 NLT

Day 75

Helpless and Weak No Longer

Dear God, sometimes it's hard to grasp all the ways Jesus' death on the cross saved me. Not only did it make a way back to You and secure eternal life in Your presence, but it also pulled me from helplessness. It made me strong rather than weak. And it has given me the courage I need to navigate some very difficult spaces in life. Your Son's selfless act of love changed me forever, and I am so grateful. Help me find that confidence every time I'm faced with fear. I don't want to be someone who cowers when adversity comes my way. Instead, I want to stand strong, empowered by Jesus' love demonstrated at Calvary. In Jesus' name I pray, amen.

For when the time was right, the Anointed One came and died to demonstrate his love for sinners who were entirely helpless, weak, and powerless to save themselves.

ROMANS 5:6 TPT

Day 76

His Hands Alone

There are times, Lord, when my troubles, my worries, my circumstances bring me so low that I have only one way to go—up. To You. You are the one I have to trust when I come to the end of myself. You are the only one who can deliver me from both troubles that come against me from others and problems I may have caused myself. I find such comfort in that knowledge, Lord. Although I know *I* will falter, I know You never will. That is why I trust in and depend on You alone, putting all I have, all I am, and all I dream to be in Your hands. In Jesus' name, amen.

We do not want you to be uninformed, brethren, about the affliction and oppressing distress which befell us in [the province of] Asia, how we were so utterly and unbearably weighed down and crushed that we despaired even of life [itself]. Indeed, we felt within ourselves that we had received the [very] sentence of death, but that was to keep us from trusting in and depending on ourselves instead of on God Who raises the dead.

2 CORINTHIANS 1:8–9 AMPC

Day 77

Free Indeed

God, I can hardly believe my good fortune as Your child! I thought that my sentence was irreversible. I've sinned. I've messed up. I'm not going to deny it, because it's true. I've done wrong in Your eyes. My punishment was not misplaced. I wasn't wrongly accused or suffering from a case of mistaken identity. I was caught red-handed with the evidence stacked against me. I deserved Your condemnation. . . .

But then a miraculous thing happened. Instead of serving an eternal sentence, locked away from You for all time, You swung Your gavel and pronounced, "Forgiven!" My dead hope sparked to life. My mind could hardly follow. I'm free! Thank You, Jesus. . .You served my sentence for me. In Your precious name, amen.

For the wages of sin is death, but the gift of God is eternal life in Christ Jesus our Lord.
ROMANS 6:23 NIV

Day 78

Strength from His Presence

Dear God, I think I'm beginning to understand that being strong and having courage is possible when I know You are with me. For so long, I've tried to gut it out myself, relying on my own strength to make myself brave. I've tried to talk myself into having courage. I've tried all the tricks of the trade, like self-care, meditation, visualization, and repeating empowering phrases. In the end, they've all left me fearful and struggling with the same insecurities. But if I take a moment to remember that Your promise is to never leave me alone, I can find confidence and courage from that powerful truth. Thank You for knowing I need You by my side. In Jesus' name I pray, amen.

Then GOD commanded Joshua son of Nun saying, "Be strong. Take courage. You will lead the People of Israel into the land I promised to give them. And I'll be right there with you."
DEUTERONOMY 31:23 MSG

Day 79

In the Land of the Living

Here I am, Lord, coming to You, resting at Your feet, waiting for the wisdom I need to see me through this day and the night that follows. I know that when I seek You, I will find You, for You care for me. You will never abandon me, lose me, or forsake me.

Lord, guide me to a smooth path, a path clearly marked out for me. Help me find the hope I've been seeking. And if I stand in a place of uncertainty, lead me to the goodness I know awaits me in the land of the living. If impatience starts to nibble at my confidence, remind me to wait for You. In the meantime, keep me strong and brave, confident Your answer is on its way. Amen.

*Lord, hear my voice when I call; be gracious to me and
answer me. . . . Show me Your way, Lord, and lead me on
a level path. . . . I am certain that I will see the
Lord's goodness in the land of the living. Wait for the
Lord; be strong and courageous. Wait for the Lord.*
Psalm 27:7, 11, 13–14 hcsb

Day 80

Gather Me Close

Jesus, I'm struggling. I'm feeling vulnerable and invisible. My strength is waning, and my stress is winning. I'm not sure I can go on like this. Does anyone see me, God? . . . Do You? Have You forsaken me? My help seems far off. . .and yet, Father, I refuse to listen to this voice in my head whispering that I'm lost to You.

I know that my ways are not hidden from Your sight. You shield the weak ones of Your flock, and You are gentle with me when I need special care. Open my eyes to the ways You are caring for me even now, because You know all my needs. Jesus, gather me gently in Your arms and carry me close to Your heart. Amen.

He tends his flock like a shepherd: He gathers the lambs in his arms and carries them close to his heart; he gently leads those that have young.

ISAIAH 40:11 NIV

Day 81

Being Confident in Plans

Dear God, today's verse is so encouraging because it empowers me to speak up and present a positive perspective. There are so many times I feel confident in moving forward but am afraid to voice it to others, especially when groupthink isn't the same as mine. Give me boldness to make a case for what I believe. Let me remember that it's okay when not everyone agrees. And help me not be discouraged by those who don't feel as confident in my plans as I do. There is grace for everyone's opinion! But I trust that if my plans are Your plans, You'll give me the favor I need to bravely take them one more step in the right direction. In Jesus' name I pray, amen.

But Caleb calmed the congregation, and he spoke
to Moses. ["]We should go straight in, right away,
and take it over. We are surely able! ["]
NUMBERS 13:30 VOICE

Day 82

Keep on Believing

I'm coming to You, Lord, laying myself and my worries at Your feet. I know You can fix anything. And so I ask You to enter into my situation, alleviate my trouble, make my circumstances clear, and guide me where You'd have me go. Help me to stop worrying and just leave all things in Your hands. For no matter what I hear from fellow humans, I know You have the final and definitive answer for me and mine. So I will muffle the voices of assumption, the feelings of fear, and zero in on Your voice alone, the voice that continually tells me, "Do not fear. Only keep on believing!"

Jairus. . .prostrated himself at His feet and begged Him earnestly, saying, My little daughter is at the point of death. Come and lay Your hands on her, so that she may be healed and live. . . . There came some from the ruler's house, who said [to Jairus], Your daughter has died. Why bother and distress the Teacher any further? Overhearing but ignoring what they said, Jesus said to the ruler of the synagogue, Do not be seized with alarm and struck with fear; only keep on believing.

MARK 5:22–23, 35–36 AMPC

Day 83

Overwhelming Victory

Lord, my enemy, Satan, wants me to believe that difficult circumstances can defeat me and steal my victory. But I will not allow my outward circumstances to rob my joy. Illness, stress, financial struggle, relationship difficulties. . .they will not drag me down into depression.

Jesus, You defeated sin and death once and for all. You handed me a victory. It's a done deal. My eternity with You is set. And Satan thinks this problem is going to defeat me? . . . I won a long time ago. *Nothing*—not disease or rejection or an empty bank account or failure or death—no, *nothing* can separate me now (or ever!) from the great love of God. Father, help me to live a victorious life. Your kingdom is here. In Jesus' name, amen.

Overwhelming victory is ours through Christ, who loved us.
Romans 8:37 nlt

Day 84

Unshakable Confidence

Dear God, the one thing that stands between me and unshakable confidence is fear. It knocks me to my knees. It undermines my gumption to try again. It talks me out of trusting that You'll help me accomplish meaningful things in my life. I'm tired of being held captive by worry and insecurity. This isn't how life should be. It's not Your best for me. And even though I have faith in You, sometimes it's not enough. From today forward, I'm going to focus on You over my fear. Every time I feel it creeping in, I'm going to pray for Your unshakable confidence to override the worry. Let that act of faith help me become secure in Your love. In Jesus' name I pray, amen.

So now, beloved ones, stand firm, stable, and enduring.
Live your lives with an unshakable confidence. We know
that we prosper and excel in every season by serving the
Lord, because we are assured that our union with the Lord
makes our labor productive with fruit that endures.

1 CORINTHIANS 15:58 TPT

Day 85

Good Success

I'm passionate about Your Word, Lord. I love soaking myself in it, talking about it, thinking about it night and day. Knowing so much about You and Your way helps me to follow You, to know the path You would have me walk. For I know that when I'm following in Your footprints, I'm heading in the right direction and things will work out well. With the wisdom of Your Word in my heart, mind, and spirit, I know I can find the strength and courage I need to do what You would have me do. With You going before me, walking beside me, and watching my back, success is ours. Amen.

This Book of the Law shall not depart out of your mouth, but you shall meditate on it day and night, that you may observe and do according to all that is written in it. For then you shall make your way prosperous, and then you shall deal wisely and have good success. Have not I commanded you? Be strong, vigorous, and very courageous. Be not afraid, neither be dismayed, for the Lord your God is with you wherever you go.

JOSHUA 1:8–9 AMPC

Day 86

Knocked Down but Not Destroyed

Lord, the light of Jesus shines in me! I am a fragile vessel full of chips and cracks, and yet I contain the greatest treasure—the life that Jesus has given me. The amazing grace You have extended to me. . .the way You love me no matter what.

I may be hard pressed. I may be perplexed and hunted, but I am not crushed; I will not despair, and I am never abandoned by You, God. I refuse to give up even if I am knocked to my knees. The power that lives in me comes from You alone, God. No one could mistake this broken pot for a superpower. Thank You, God, for allowing me to see and know You in the face of Jesus. Amen.

We now have this light shining in our hearts, but we ourselves are like fragile clay jars containing this great treasure. This makes it clear that our great power is from God, not from ourselves. We are pressed on every side by troubles, but we are not crushed. We are perplexed, but not driven to despair. We are hunted down, but never abandoned by God. We get knocked down, but we are not destroyed.

2 CORINTHIANS 4:7–9 NLT

Day 87

A Sliver of Faith

Dear God, I know the way to overcome fear is to anchor my faith in You. I know Your Word says that even a sliver of faith can do mighty things in me and through me. The problem is I worry that the little bit I have is not enough. When my relationships turn rocky, I cower in concern. When my finances or health start to spiral, I'm sidelined by the stress. I rarely stand tall when I'm scared. And it seems my spark of faith isn't worth the effort. Help me remember that faith as tiny as a mustard seed has power to undo fear. You'll honor my willingness to trust You, no matter how big or small. In Jesus' name I pray, amen.

Because you have so little faith. I tell you this: if you had even a faint spark of faith, even faith as tiny as a mustard seed, you could say to this mountain, "Move from here to there," and because of your faith, the mountain would move. If you had just a sliver of faith, you would find nothing impossible.
MATTHEW 17:20 VOICE

Day 88

Champion of the Faithful

The wonders You've performed so that Your faithful could go where You told them to go are stupendous. But each of those wonders was performed only *after* Your people did what You commanded them to do—no matter how strange, questionable, or unreasonable they thought Your directions were at the time! When Your people seemed to be stuck between the Egyptians and the Red Sea and all seemed lost, You parted the sea. You brought down the walls of Jericho after Your people spent seven days marching around them. And You used a woman of ill repute to help Your spies—and that same woman and her family—escape destruction. That is why all my hope and trust lie in You, the champion of the faithful. Amen.

By an act of faith, Israel walked through the Red Sea on dry ground. The Egyptians tried it and drowned. By faith, the Israelites marched around the walls of Jericho for seven days, and the walls fell flat. By an act of faith, Rahab, the Jericho harlot, welcomed the spies and escaped the destruction that came on those who refused to trust God.

HEBREWS 11:29–31 MSG

Day 89

Weapon-Wielding Woman

God, we are not defenseless in this world. We are far from having no protection. You've outfitted us with divine weapons for our fight in this war with eternal consequences. We can walk confidently, because the secret to our joy and security is that this war is already won.

Satan is a defeated foe who wants to keep us from living in the victory we possess today. Our enemy wants to keep us from knowing You and deceive us into believing lies about You. But You have given us faith as our shield against hopelessness, salvation as a helmet over our minds, the righteousness of Jesus as our body armor, truth to belt it all together, and Your Spirit and Your Word to engage the enemy in combat. Thank You, Father! Amen.

We are human, but we don't wage war as humans do. We use
God's mighty weapons, not worldly weapons, to knock
down the strongholds of human reasoning and to destroy
false arguments. We destroy every proud obstacle that
keeps people from knowing God. We capture their
rebellious thoughts and teach them to obey Christ.

2 Corinthians 10:3–5 NLT

Day 90

The Next Step

Dear God, help me take this next step in faith. I know You're asking me to tread way out of my comfort zone to do something new, and it's terrifying. My heart is anxious at the thought of what's next. I can relate to Esther in today's verses, feeling like there's a possibility for things to go wrong. But like her, I am also fully resolved to follow Your leading. Would You please fill me with courage as I say yes to Your prompting? Shine Your favor on my efforts. Bless me with strategy and creativity. Open the right doors along the way. And give me the courage to take the next step in faith with You. In Jesus' name I pray, amen.

> *Esther sent back her answer to Mordecai: "Go and get all the Jews living in Susa together. Fast for me. Don't eat or drink for three days, either day or night. I and my maids will fast with you. If you will do this, I'll go to the king, even though it's forbidden. If I die, I die."*
> ESTHER 4:15–16 MSG

Day 91

What a Plan

Some days, Lord, I'm not sure if I'm in the right place or if I've made the right decision. I look around me and wonder where I've been, where I am, and where I might be going. I start worrying that maybe I should be doing something else, living somewhere else, loving someone else. Then, when I finally quiet myself, I hear Your voice reminding me that You have plans for me, plans for my good, to give me hope and a future. That all I need to do is call on You, run to You, pray to You, and You will hear my voice. That when I seek You—with all my heart—You will be found and my fortunes restored. What a Lord! What a promise! What a plan!

"I know the plans I have for you, declares the LORD, plans for welfare and not for evil, to give you a future and a hope. Then you will call upon me and come and pray to me, and I will hear you. You will seek me and find me, when you seek me with all your heart. I will be found by you, declares the LORD, and I will restore your fortunes."

JEREMIAH 29:11–14 ESV

Day 92

His Tender Call

Heavenly Father, I'm guilty of forgetting You as I pursued other loves in my life. I indulged my desires and ignored Your voice. At times I have consciously chosen sin over righteousness. I have led myself into a stressed-out mess of my own making.

And yet You didn't criticize me for my foolishness or judge me for my mistakes. Instead You chose to woo me back with gentle words. You led me to a quiet place to be alone with You—to focus only on You. Father, may I never again forget Your goodness to me. I desire faithfulness to You, who are ever faithful to me. I will praise You even in the wilderness, because out of Your deep love, You turn my troubles into hope. Amen.

> "She decked herself with rings and jewelry, and went after her lovers, but me she forgot," declares the LORD. "Therefore I am now going to allure her; I will lead her into the wilderness and speak tenderly to her. There I will give her back her vineyards, and will make the Valley of Achor a door of hope. There she will respond as in the days of her youth."
>
> HOSEA 2:13–15 NIV

Day 93

The Future

Dear God, let me find peace in trusting You know the details of my life. I don't have to fear the unknown because my future is known. I don't have to be scared because You're already there. What a blessing that I can find rest in Your sovereignty. Thank You for going before me and making plans. That frees me to live in confidence, certain I'll not fall. I believe You have planned peace and not evil for me. That doesn't mean an easy and pain-free life, but it gives hope for the final outcome of my life. It means it will all work out for my benefit and Your glory. I can live with that! In Jesus' name I pray, amen.

For I know the thoughts and plans that I have for you, says the Lord, thoughts and plans for welfare and peace and not for evil, to give you hope in your final outcome.
JEREMIAH 29:11 AMPC

Day 94

His Capable Hands

Lord, like this verse warns, a tornado of plans spins through my mind, battering my weary brain. But it is Your plan that comes to pass. All my striving is for nothing if I am living outside of Your good plans for me.

Relieve my stress as I open my hands and release my plans and problems to Your capable hands. The reality of my situation is that I don't have control—I never did. I only thought that I could make things happen all on my own. But everything that You set out to do, Father, happens in a big way. You have the power. Please help me to recognize Your plans and to lay aside the ideas that are mine and mine alone. Amen.

*Many are the plans in a person's heart, but it
is the LORD's purpose that prevails.*
PROVERBS 19:21 NIV

Day 95

Restored

Jesus, I have a chronic issue. One I can't seem to get relief from. I feel like the woman with the issue of blood. I've heard about You. I know what You can do for Your children. I keep telling myself that if I can just touch You, reach out and connect with You heart-to-heart, I will be healed. You will say to me, "Daughter, your confidence in Me has restored you. Now go in peace." So here I am, Lord. I'm coming to You, stretching out to touch the hem of Your garment, knowing You can heal all, waiting for Your power to flow into me. . .knowing my faith in You will restore me.

There was a woman who had had a flow of blood for twelve
years. . . . She had heard the reports concerning Jesus,
and she came up behind Him in the throng and touched His
garment, for she kept saying, If I only touch His garments,
I shall be restored to health. And immediately her flow of
blood was dried up at the source, and [suddenly] she felt in
her body that she was healed of her [distressing] ailment.

MARK 5:25, 27–29 AMPC

Day 96

Overwhelming Feelings

Dear God, sometimes grief feels so heavy I'm afraid I'll never have peace. I get lost in sadness and hopelessness. And rather than see any light at the end of the tunnel, I just want to curl up in bed and pull the covers over my head. But You're clear in saying that if I choose to keep my mind on You, pressing in for hope and joy, then You'll keep me in perfect and constant peace. That means when those worrisome feelings flood my heart and I pray about it, You'll remove the heaviness. It means if I make You my default when grief overwhelms me, the intensity of emotions will be lifted and replaced with peace. In Jesus' name I pray, amen.

You will guard him and keep him in perfect and constant peace whose mind [both its inclination and its character] is stayed on You, because he commits himself to You, leans on You, and hopes confidently in You.
ISAIAH 26:3 AMPC

Day 97

Know Him

God, it's stunning to realize that You, the God of all creation, the beginning and the end, want to know me and be known by me. You desired a relationship even with a stubborn people who often walked away from every good thing You offered them, instead running after whatever seemed like a good idea at the time. You called out and revealed Yourself. You pleaded with them to choose You over every other empty thing that held them captivated.

Father, how much of my stress comes from walking right past Your outstretched hand that offers abundant life, and instead pursuing my own imagination? I see now how much You miss me when I'm far from You. Keep me close, Father. Amen.

"I revealed myself to those who did not ask for me; I was found by those who did not seek me. To a nation that did not call on my name, I said, 'Here am I, here am I.' All day long I have held out my hands to an obstinate people, who walk in ways not good, pursuing their own imaginations."

Isaiah 65:1–2 NIV

Day 98

Helping Others

Dear God, please fill me with courage to reach out to others who are in need of help. It's so much easier to stay comfortable within my community than to be Your hands and feet to those around me. Maybe it's because I feel ill equipped. Maybe it's because I'm afraid of messing something up. Maybe it's because I'm worried about my personal safety. Regardless, I could use a dose of divine courage to connect with those in need and show them Your love. Give me the spiritual eyes to see where I can step in and help. Open my heart to being generous with my time. And remove any fear that keeps me tucked away in my comfort zone. In Jesus' name I pray, amen.

This is how we've come to understand and experience love: Christ sacrificed his life for us. This is why we ought to live sacrificially for our fellow believers, and not just be out for ourselves. If you see some brother or sister in need and have the means to do something about it but turn a cold shoulder and do nothing, what happens to God's love? It disappears. And you made it disappear.
1 JOHN 3:16–17 MSG

Day 99

My Part

So many times, Lord, You tell me that You are with me, will never fail nor leave me. And that my part is to be strong, to be brave, to do all You tell me to do. You tell me I should never deviate from Your Word and the path it urges me to take. You say if I do all that, I will prosper wherever I go. It sounds easy, Lord, but it's not. Sometimes You may be with me, but I move off course. I fail to see You—sometimes I even fail to look for You. Then I find myself becoming fearful and losing confidence. So, Lord, remind me every day of my part. And I'll take courage knowing Yours.

I will be with you; I will not fail you or forsake you. Be strong (confident) and of good courage, for you shall cause this people to inherit the land which I swore to their fathers to give them. Only you be strong and very courageous, that you may do according to all the law which Moses My servant commanded you. Turn not from it to the right hand or to the left, that you may prosper wherever you go.
JOSHUA 1:5–7 AMPC

Day 100

A New Name

Father in heaven, the enemy whispers lies into my ear. He tries to defeat me by saying that I'm unworthy, unwanted, unloved, forgotten. He tells me that I'm nothing. He tells me that I'm hopeless.

But when my stress and anxiety begin to assault me, I choose to ignore his poisonous murmurs. Instead I choose to listen to Your Word. And You have promised me a new name. You say that I am cherished. Loved. Known. Forgiven. Accepted. You say I'm Yours. And to the victorious, You promise a white stone inscribed with a special name from You. God, give me victory today, because I want to hold one of those precious white stones when You return. Amen.

To the one who is victorious, I will give some of the hidden manna. I will also give that person a white stone with a new name written on it, known only to the one who receives it.

REVELATION 2:17 NIV

Day 101

Love Yourself

Dear God, I'm not very kind to myself. I criticize and beat myself up on the regular, unable to give myself a break. It seems my expectations are over the top and hold me to a standard I can never live up to. At the root is a worry that I'll never be good enough in the eyes of others, which makes me extra tough on myself. But today's scripture reveals the power of Your love. It tells me that You are greater than my anxious heart. It says You know more about me than I do. And honestly, if You can love me after seeing all my imperfections, certainly I can find the courage to be unafraid to love myself too. In Jesus' name I pray, amen.

My dear children, let's not just talk about love; let's practice real love. This is the only way we'll know we're living truly, living in God's reality. It's also the way to shut down debilitating self-criticism, even when there is something to it. For God is greater than our worried hearts and knows more about us than we do ourselves.

1 John 3:18–20 msg

Day 102

By the Help of Faith

I'm amazed, Lord, by what You can accomplish through Your people. Even though I'm only one person, prompted and empowered by my faith in You, I too can obtain the promises with which You've blessed us. I can close the mouths of roaring predators, put out the flames of evil, escape those who come against me, and become mighty and invincible when fighting for Your good. With You within me, going before me, walking beside me, and watching over me, I cannot lose. Any worries that I've been entertaining—both large and small—are vanquished by my faith and trust in You, leaving me with only one question. What would You have me do today in Your name? Amen.

Time would fail me to tell of Gideon, Barak, Samson, Jephthah, of David and Samuel and the prophets, who by [the help of] faith subdued kingdoms, administered justice, obtained promised blessings, closed the mouths of lions, extinguished the power of raging fire, escaped the devourings of the sword, out of frailty and weakness won strength and became stalwart, even mighty and resistless in battle, routing alien hosts.

HEBREWS 11:32–34 AMPC

Day 103

Compassionate Savior

Father, I've entertained the wrong impression of who You are. I thought that You condemned me, that I had to be perfect in order to be accepted by You. And I was so tired, stressed, and hopeless, because no matter how hard I tried to live up to Your expectations, in the end I always failed. I sinned. . .over and over and over. I told myself countless times that tomorrow would be different, tomorrow I would succeed, but I didn't.

But then I learned about what Jesus did for me—I was introduced to Your amazing grace! I learned that You don't look at me with censure and anger and impatience. You see me with compassion. Thank You, God, for Your grace. Amen.

When he saw the crowds, he felt compassion for them,
because they were distressed and dejected,
like sheep without a shepherd.
MATTHEW 9:36 CSB

Day 104

The Power of Together

Dear God, give me courage against the enemy. Your Word paints a powerful image of him roaming and looking for someone to devour. Rather than make me afraid, may that visual strengthen me to be alert, knowing his plans are to discourage and distract. With Your help, I can activate my faith and stand strong against him. I may be facing a hard situation, but I'm not alone. There are others facing many of the same circumstances. Somehow that deeply encourages me to resist any and all of the enemy's plans. There is power in numbers! And in You, we have all the power we need as a community of believers to stand strong in faith and be conquerors! In Jesus' name I pray, amen.

*Be well balanced and always alert, because your enemy,
the devil, roams around incessantly, like a roaring lion looking
for its prey to devour. Take a decisive stand against him and
resist his every attack with strong, vigorous faith. For you
know that your believing brothers and sisters around the world
are experiencing the same kinds of troubles you endure.*
1 PETER 5:8–9 TPT

Day 105

Your Rescuing Knight

Growing up, I heard a lot of fairy tales about princesses being rescued. But that was far from my reality until I met You. For You, Lord, are my prince, my knight in shining armor. You're the rock I stand on, the castle in which I dwell, the one I run to when I'm afraid and want to hide. You're my fortress, the place where no one can reach me. So to You I'll sing my praise, for You are the real thing. When I'm in trouble and call out to You, I know You'll not only hear me but bring me straight into Your presence, safe and sound. What a knight! Amen.

God is bedrock under my feet, the castle in which I live, my rescuing knight. My God—the high crag where I run for dear life, hiding behind the boulders, safe in the granite hideout; my mountaintop refuge, he saves me from ruthless men. I sing to God the Praise-Lofty, and find myself safe and saved. . . . A hostile world! I called to God, to my God I cried out. From his palace he heard me call; my cry brought me right into his presence—a private audience!

2 Samuel 22:2–4, 7 msg

Day 106

Fill Me Up

Lord, when someone asks how we are, the answer is usually some tired version of stressed out, worn out, or down and out. But I'm done with hopeless living. I want to be filled with something better than frazzled emotions and a frenzied lifestyle. I want to be filled to the brim with You. I want to shout as the psalmist did, "My cup runneth over!"

Father, please fill me with Your love, grace, peace, and joy until they flow over my brim, delighting all those around me. May my spirit no longer be filled with complaints but instead overflow with all the fullness of the power of Your Holy Spirit. In Jesus' name, amen.

*May the God of hope fill you with all joy and peace
as you trust in him, so that you may overflow with
hope by the power of the Holy Spirit.*
ROMANS 15:13 NIV

Day 107

Clear Thinking

Dear God, help me keep my mind clear and use common sense when I start to fear. Give me wisdom to see exactly what's causing the anxiety. Give me discernment to know if my fears are founded in truth or lies. I don't want to waste my one and only life running away and cowering from something that's not real. I don't want to give in to worries that are baseless. Please bless me with spiritual eyes to know the truth so I can live in freedom. Make me strong in my faith as I trust in You to guide and protect me. Build my confidence in who You say I am. And give me courage to brave whatever comes! In Jesus' name I pray, amen.

Dear friend, guard Clear Thinking and Common Sense with your life; don't for a minute lose sight of them. They'll keep your soul alive and well, they'll keep you fit and attractive. You'll travel safely, you'll neither tire nor trip. You'll take afternoon naps without a worry, you'll enjoy a good night's sleep.
PROVERBS 3:21–24 MSG

Day 108

God of My Details

Father, why do I allow worries and fears to run me ragged when I am resting in the care of the good shepherd—the one who loves me more than I could ever imagine or comprehend? You notice when a sparrow falls—a tiny, ubiquitous bird that everyone overlooks. . .everyone except You. And You take so much care that You've even numbered the hairs on my head.

Father, if You notice when a single strand slips from my head, no detail escapes Your watchful eye. You supply everything that I need, exactly when I need it. I want to trust You more. You're pleased to give good things to Your children, Father—including me. Thank You for taking care of every aspect of my life. In Jesus' name, amen.

"Aren't five sparrows sold for two pennies? Yet not one of them is forgotten in God's sight. Indeed, the hairs of your head are all counted. Don't be afraid; you are worth more than many sparrows."
LUKE 12:6–7 CSB

Day 109

No Need to Panic

Dear God, when panic begins to set in, my emotions usually spiral out of control. My mind goes in a million different directions as I try to make sense of what's just happened. I struggle to form a clear thought. And rather than take a deep breath, take a step back, and ask You to bring clarity, I end up in a hot mess. When that happens, it's because I've forgotten You are with me in that moment. I've forgotten Your presence enables me to be strong and courageous. I may be caught off guard initially, but my next response should be one of peace and trust. Fear has no hold because trusting You brings peace instead. In Jesus' name I pray, amen.

No need to panic over alarms or surprises, or predictions that doomsday's just around the corner, because GOD will be right there with you; he'll keep you safe and sound.
PROVERBS 3:25–26 MSG

Day 110

Press On

Lord, every time I turn back and get hung up on the past, worrying about what I could have or should have done back then, I end up stumbling on my path. So I'm coming to You for help. Help me to stop focusing on the past. Help me to forget what has gone before. I know that although I can't change the past, I can do better in the present and look forward to what lies ahead. Fill me, Lord God, with the energy, strength, power, and wisdom to press on. For my goal, my aim, is to reach the end of this journey and obtain that wonderful prize to which You, through Jesus, are calling me. In His wonderful name I pray, amen.

I press on to possess that perfection for which Christ Jesus
first possessed me. No, dear brothers and sisters, I have
not achieved it, but I focus on this one thing: Forgetting
the past and looking forward to what lies ahead, I press on
to reach the end of the race and receive the heavenly prize
for which God, through Christ Jesus, is calling us.
PHILIPPIANS 3:12–14 NLT

Day 111

Held by Him

Lord, a little child falls and scrapes her knee and then climbs into her papa's lap just to snuggle—she's content to sit wrapped in the gentle arms of someone who loves her, someone who will soothe away the pain. No matter our age, we all want the same things—comfort, the assurance that it will be well again. Sometimes we don't want words or advice or answers. . .we just need a hug, a connection that communicates love and caring and lets us know that we're okay.

Thank You, Jesus, that I can run into Your tender and strong arms when I need to be held. I find comfort in the assurance of Your love and compassion, Your strength and control. In Jesus' name, amen.

Blessed be the God and Father of our Lord Jesus Christ,
the Father of mercies and the God of all comfort.
He comforts us in all our affliction, so that we may be
able to comfort those who are in any kind of affliction,
through the comfort we ourselves receive from God.
2 Corinthians 1:3–4 csb

Day 112

Courage in Changes

Dear God, even though Your Word says there are different seasons in life, it's hard for me to accept change. I like comfort and predictability, and I get stirred up when I'm faced with change. It makes me nervous. The unknown is a hard place for me to navigate. Please bring peace to my heart and remind me that You never change. Remind me that there is never a season in life that I'll have to walk through without You. And give me the courage to accept that change is a natural, normal, and good part of life. Even more, make me confident in knowing You're already in those new places making a way for me. In Jesus' name I pray, amen.

For everything that happens in life—there is a season,
a right time for everything under heaven. . .a time to tear apart,
a time to bind together; a time to be quiet, a time to speak up;
a time to love, a time to hate; a time to go
to war, a time to make peace.
ECCLESIASTES 3:1, 7–8 VOICE

Day 113

God Goes before You

Over and over again I need to hear Your words telling me to be strong, to have courage, and to stand firm. Because, Lord, You have promised You not only will go with me but will never fail me. Nor will You forsake me. And at the same time You're going before me, checking things out before I get there, You are also marching with me! Only You, God, can be in every place at the same time, making sure I come to no harm. Your presence gives me the confidence I need, the calm I crave, and the joy my heart cries out for. Thank You, Lord, for Your empowering presence and so much more. Amen.

Be strong, courageous, and firm; fear not nor be in terror before them, for it is the Lord your God Who goes with you; He will not fail you or forsake you. . . . Be strong, courageous, and firm. . . . It is the Lord Who goes before you; He will [march] with you; He will not fail you or let you go or forsake you; [let there be no cowardice or flinching, but] fear not, neither become broken [in spirit—depressed, dismayed, and unnerved with alarm].
DEUTERONOMY 31:6–8 AMPC

Day 114

My Help

God, we humans are stubborn and independent creatures. I shake my head at my own pride. I find it far too difficult to admit my inadequacies to myself, so forget asking for help when I need it.

Father, show me where my stubborn pride has become a source of anxiety and stress. I know that, ultimately, my help comes from You. And I need to remember that sometimes You also work through the hands of my brothers and sisters in Christ. By rejecting their help, I am robbing them of the opportunity to bless others. Teach me to be humble and gracious in accepting help and blessings from others—and strengthen me, so that in return I can also assist those in need. Amen.

I lift my eyes toward the mountains. Where will my help come from? My help comes from the LORD, the Maker of heaven and earth. He will not allow your foot to slip; you Protector will not slumber. Indeed, the Protector of Israel does not slumber or sleep.
PSALM 121:1–4 CSB

Day 115

Peace That Calms Anxiety

Dear God, how am I supposed to not worry about things? When my kids are stressing me out and my marriage is on divorce's doorstep, how can I be calm? When I'm falling behind at work and the boss is noticing, how can I rest? When my insecurities overwhelm me and I'm struggling to like myself, how am I supposed to be okay? You say being saturated in prayer is key, but I'm not convinced. Help me give it a shot. Every time fear creeps in, remind me to talk to You about it. Let me share everything down to the minute details of my worry. Show up, Lord. Give me the peace I so desperately need to calm my anxiety. In Jesus' name I pray, amen.

Don't be pulled in different directions or worried about a thing. Be saturated in prayer throughout each day, offering your faith-filled requests before God with overflowing gratitude. Tell him every detail of your life, then God's wonderful peace that transcends human understanding, will guard your heart and mind through Jesus Christ.

PHILIPPIANS 4:6–7 TPT

Day 116

"Doing" the Word

I admit it, Lord. Sometimes I get into a slump, just half-heartedly reading Your Word but not doing anything with it. Then I wonder why I feel untethered or have trouble focusing. So help me, Lord, not just to listen to what You have to say through Your Word, but to actually do what it says. Remind me that Your Word shows me the truth, and that truth is what will set me free. Help me keep in mind that when I do what You say and remember what I've heard, You will bless me. In Jesus' name, amen.

Don't just listen to God's word. You must do what it says.
Otherwise, you are only fooling yourselves. For if you listen
to the word and don't obey, it is like glancing at your face
in a mirror. You see yourself, walk away, and forget what
you look like. But if you look carefully into the perfect law
that sets you free, and if you do what it says and don't forget
what you heard, then God will bless you for doing it.
JAMES 1:22–25 NLT

Day 117

My Good Father

Father, this world can feel like it's imploding with chaos. My stress clenches a tight fist around my heart because life seems dark, dangerous, and unpredictable. I question Your good intent and worry about a future that looks so uncertain.

But thank You, God, for the reminder that You are good. Darkness cannot dwell in Your unadulterated light. Your love endures forever, and You love me as Your own precious child. I belong to You, and You shelter me and fill me with unsurpassed peace and hope of an eternal future with You. I may not always understand Your ways, because I know they are infinitely higher than mine, but I trust in Your love and goodwill toward me. In Jesus' name, amen.

They celebrate your abundant goodness and joyfully
sing of your righteousness. The LORD is gracious and
compassionate, slow to anger and rich in love. The LORD
is good to all; he has compassion on all he has made.
PSALM 145:7–9 NIV

Day 118

The Greatest Teacher

Lord, there are days when I seem to lose my footing. Some people have strange ideas of what it means to be a Christian. They teach things that don't seem to be in line with Your Word. And then they act on those teachings. Knowing how to respond to these people and their strange ideas can be confusing.

So help me, Lord, to stick with Your Word and keep to Your true way. Help me not to be like some babe in the woods who doesn't know the first thing about what it means to be a woman of Christ. Help me not to be influenced by those who are not of You. And above all, help me to speak Your truth in love. For I want to become more like Your Son, Jesus Christ, who is the greatest teacher of all. Amen.

Then we will no longer be immature like children. We won't be tossed and blown about by every wind of new teaching. We will not be influenced when people try to trick us with lies so clever they sound like the truth. Instead, we will speak the truth in love, growing in every way more and more like Christ, who is the head of his body, the church.

EPHESIANS 4:14–15 NLT

Day 119

I Am New

God, I'm here on my knees before You, the holy one, to confess that I am broken. What's worse is I look around and realize that the whole world is broken and torn up by sin—hatred and war, abuse of the weak, hurting families, extreme selfishness masquerading as love. I've tried to fix this brokenness, but the effort has left me depleted.

I can't make right the problems and suffering in this place any more than I can mend the sin in my own life. I need You, Jesus. When I surrendered to You, an amazing thing happened. You made me new! You reconciled all the wrongs and healed my broken places. Give me boldness in sharing this message of reconciliation with the broken people I meet. Amen.

Therefore, if anyone is in Christ, the new creation has come:
The old has gone, the new is here! All this is from God,
who reconciled us to himself through Christ and gave us the
ministry of reconciliation: that God was reconciling the world
to himself in Christ, not counting people's sins against them.
And he has committed to us the message of reconciliation.
2 CORINTHIANS 5:17–19 NIV

Day 120

It's Not Up to You

Dear God, sometimes I put pressure on myself to make everything work out for the best. I decide good and beneficial outcomes depend on my time and effort, so I push to be a playmaker and save the day. It's exhausting. And honestly, all that focus rarely yields the results I was hoping for anyway. There's freedom in remembering that every good and perfect gift comes from You. I don't have to be God because You are. My job is to be obedient to Your leadership and to trust Your will and ways. Anytime I feel afraid or worried that I can't fix or control something, let it be a red flag to surrender it to You. In Jesus' name I pray, amen.

Every good gift, every perfect gift, comes from above.
These gifts come down from the Father, the creator of the
heavenly lights, in whose character there is no change at all.

JAMES 1:17 CEB

Day 121

God's Help

In these troubled times, Lord, help me not to look around me in terror but rather to look to You only. For, standing with You, I have nothing to fear.

You are the God of all gods. You are the one who gives me the strength I need to bear up. You remind me of past difficulties I've had and how You got me through. You not only help me but hold me up and keep me safe. You promise to protect me from anything that comes against me. You'll keep me safe as You hold my hand and say, "Don't fear, little one. I'm here. And I'll help." Amen.

Fear not [there is nothing to fear], for I am with you; do not look around you in terror and be dismayed, for I am your God. I will strengthen and harden you to difficulties, yes, I will help you; yes, I will hold you up and retain you with My [victorious] right hand of rightness and justice. . . . For I the Lord your God hold your right hand; I am the Lord, Who says to you, Fear not; I will help you!
ISAIAH 41:10, 13 AMPC

Day 122

Thrive beside the Water

Heavenly Father, the scorched and dusty wasteland around me seems hostile to tender new growth. I want to stand firm, but I don't always. Sometimes my brittle branches snap under the stress of my trials. But You have a better vision for me.

Father, when I twine my roots deeply into the living water of Your Word every day, I thrive in a parched world. My branches grow heavy with the succulent fruit of Your Spirit. Not only do I stand firm and prosper despite harsh conditions but others are drawn to the fruit of my fellowship with You, Jesus. They see peace amid turmoil, joy in struggles, patience in hardship, and deep love. May my fruit draw others to Your living water that sustains me. Amen.

Blessed is the one who does not walk in step with the wicked or stand in the way that sinners take or sit in the company of mockers, but whose delight is in the law of the LORD, and who meditates on his law day and night. That person is like a tree planted by streams of water, which yields its fruit in season and whose leaf does not wither—whatever they do prospers.

PSALM 1:1–3 NIV

Day 123

Key to Peace

No matter what happens, Lord, I want to be full of joy! The joy that is found in You alone. So I'm looking to learn from You, Lord, how not to worry. Instead, I want to pray about anything and everything—no matter how tremendous, how terrible, or how trivial it seems. I want to lay all my concerns at Your feet, tell You what I need to go forward, and thank You for everything You have done for me. For I know that only then will I have some idea of what Your peace is like. Only then will Your peace become a protective barrier, guarding my heart and mind as I live in Jesus the Christ, my key to peace.

Always be full of joy in the Lord. I say it again—rejoice! . . .
Don't worry about anything; instead, pray about every-
thing. Tell God what you need, and thank him for all he
has done. Then you will experience God's peace, which
exceeds anything we can understand. His peace will guard
your hearts and minds as you live in Christ Jesus.
PHILIPPIANS 4:4, 6–7 NLT

Day 124

Cup of Blessing

Lord, in the psalms David often poured out his emotions to You. It's a comfort to know that I too can confide in You. My feelings are not too much for You to handle, and You're never shocked by what churns inside me.

But help me to remember that sometimes my overwhelming emotions can be deceiving. I need to fall back on the promises of Your Word to sustain me—that You are good, loving, faithful, merciful, and strong. Allow my thoughts to tarry on my blessings instead of my complaints. My enemy would distract me with my stress and disappointments, but I choose to believe that You are my cup of blessing, and I have a beautiful inheritance. Indeed the lines have fallen for me in pleasant places. Amen.

Lord, you are my portion and my cup of blessing; you hold my future. The boundary lines have fallen for me in pleasant places; indeed, I have a beautiful inheritance. I will bless the Lord who counsels me—even at night when my thoughts trouble me.

Psalm 16:5–7 csb

Day 125

The Wait

Dear God, help me be brave as I wait for You. I'm in a tough place right now and desperate for You to intervene. I need to know You will fix this. I need to know You won't leave me stuck in this place. It's hard to sit and wait because my fear gets in the way. I worry that You are too busy, that You have forgotten me, that I'm being punished, or that my expectations of You are too high. I'm surrendering my fears and asking for supernatural patience as I wait for Your plan to unfold in this situation. I'm struggling to stay calm and hold on to peace. Give me courage to sit and wait. In Jesus' name I pray, amen.

Now the Lord is not slow about enacting His promise—slow is how some people want to characterize it—no, He is not slow but patient and merciful to you, not wanting anyone to be destroyed, but wanting everyone to turn away from following his own path and to turn toward God's.

2 PETER 3:9 VOICE

Day 126

Not Too Much for God

Father, like Moses', my life has not been smooth. Circumstances beyond my control have stacked against me, and I've made some poor choices that have negatively impacted my life. People around me often step back from the complicated issues and stress that my life seems to add to theirs because they feel that I am just too much to deal with.

But You have shown me, God, that I am not too much for You. My problems and mistakes are never too big for You to turn around. You created me *on* purpose, and You made me *for* a purpose. Please take all my past experiences, good and bad, and redeem them for Your kingdom. Thank You, Jesus, for showing me that I matter in Your kingdom. Amen.

But I have raised you up for this very purpose, that I might show you my power and that my name might be proclaimed in all the earth.
EXODUS 9:16 NIV

Day 127

Fear of Being Overlooked

Dear God, I know I'm too concerned with what others think of me. I realize that trying to fit in will only leave me emotionally bankrupt, depressed, and discouraged. But I worry that if I don't make an effort to stay relevant, I won't have any friends. People won't want to include me, and I'll struggle to find community. I'm afraid I'll be overlooked at every turn. You address this struggle, pointing to the value of being transformed from the inside out. Please transform my mind so I'll see my life from the right perspective. Please empower me to see my value and like myself. And please give me discernment to know what is and is not important in life. In Jesus' name I pray, amen.

Stop imitating the ideals and opinions of the culture around you, but be inwardly transformed by the Holy Spirit through a total reformation of how you think. This will empower you to discern God's will as you live a beautiful life, satisfying and perfect in his eyes.

ROMANS 12:2 TPT

Day 128

Safely Cradled

You, Lord, have always answered my prayers for help. So I call upon You now. I ask You to help me overcome a fretful mind. You've freed me from so many traps in the past, and I ask You to do so again.

Hear my prayer, giver of all things. Imbue me with the peace that surpasses all understanding. Replace my fretting with the joy I find in You alone. Enlighten my mind and lighten my heart. Help me trust in You alone. For then I will have the peace I yearn for. The calm I need in mind, body, spirit, and soul. The quiet confidence I require so I can both lie down and sleep, cradled in Your arms of safety. Amen.

You have freed me when I was hemmed in and enlarged me when I was in distress; have mercy upon me and hear my prayer. . . . You have put more joy and rejoicing in my heart than [they know] when their wheat and new wine have yielded abundantly. In peace I will both lie down and sleep, for You, Lord, alone make me dwell in safety and confident trust.

PSALM 4:1, 7–8 AMPC

Day 129

Trade Worry for Praise

Father, why do I allow my worries and fears to take root in my thoughts? I know that when I dwell on my insecurities, they morph into anxiety, and my anxiety grows into stress.

Today, instead of allowing such destructive thoughts to get a stranglehold on my emotions, I choose to praise You for Your wondrous attributes. I come before Your altar, God, and I realize that *You* are my greatest joy. As I dwell on Your promises and the way You have kept Your Word throughout the ages, I realize just how capable You are of managing every issue that causes me stress and how absurd it seems for me to wring my hands when You are in charge. My peace and hope rest in You. Amen.

Then I will come to the altar of God, to God, my greatest joy.
I will praise you with the lyre, God, my God. Why, my soul, are
you so dejected? Why are you in such turmoil? Put your hope
in God, for I will still praise him, my Savior and my God.
PSALM 43:4–5 CSB

Day 130

Pour Out

Dear God, I am underwater with all the stress in my life. It's one thing after another, and I cannot get on top of my fear and anxiety. Every day, I am struggling to concentrate and focus, and it's too much. Rather than feel hopeful, I battle against complete discouragement. I want to do what the Word says and pour out all my worries and stresses on You, but that's a terrifying proposition. It's such a vulnerable act. And part of me worries it may overwhelm You. Help me trust that You tenderly care for me. Mature my faith to believe it. And grow my courage to override the fear that threatens me. In Jesus' name I pray, amen.

Pour out all your worries and stress upon him and leave them there, for he always tenderly cares for you.

1 PETER 5:7 TPT

Day 131

Dwelling Places

What a relief, Lord, to know that You have gone before me to prepare a special place for me. A place where I can live with You forever. That during and after this life, You and I can have unbroken companionship with each other.

People have let me down before, left me by the wayside. But I know that is not Your way. That is not how You deal with Your loved ones. So in these days, Lord, help me not to worry but to hang on to the hope that wherever You are, I also can be, not just now but forevermore. Amen.

Do not let your hearts be troubled (distressed, agitated).
You believe in and adhere to and trust in and rely on God;
believe in and adhere to and trust in and rely also on Me.
In My Father's house there are many dwelling places (homes).
If it were not so, I would have told you; for I am going away
to prepare a place for you. . . . I will come back again and
will take you to Myself, that where I am you may be also.

JOHN 14:1–3 AMPC

Day 132

Keep On!

Father, this world questions my sanity when I say that I trust You. They look at one piece of the puzzle, one instant in time, one hurt, and say, "How can God care about us when He allows *this*?" But I know that You have a bigger picture in mind. You plan eternally. And I am going to stick with You even during the trials when I don't fully understand what You are doing. I'm not going to quit. I'm going to stay with You, God.

I'm putting all my eggs in one basket—Yours. Why? Because I see evidence of Your goodness all around me. I'm going to wait for You. I'm going to keep on trusting You for the rest of my life. Amen.

I'm sure now I'll see God's goodness in the
exuberant earth. Stay with GOD! Take heart.
Don't quit. I'll say it again: Stay with GOD.
PSALM 27:13–14 MSG

Day 133

Worrywart Training

Dear God, I come from a long line of worrywarts. As far back as I can remember, my family has been full of anxiety-ridden women, so I come by it innocently. I grew up learning to be afraid of everything. I was taught to expect the worst in others and predict horrible outcomes in situations. There was always something to be concerned about. That cup-half-empty mindset has followed me into adulthood, and I am ready to be free from it. Help me live in freedom and with hope, knowing You will fulfill every promise to take care of my every need. I don't have to live in fear or defeat because You won't let me fall. In Jesus' name I pray, amen.

Here is the bottom line: do not worry about your life.
Don't worry about what you will eat or what you will drink.
Don't worry about how you clothe your body. Living is about more
than merely eating, and the body is about more than dressing up.
MATTHEW 6:25 VOICE

Day 134

Inner Light

Lord, I'm looking for a calm life. But to get there, I need Your help. So I ask You, Lord, to help me curb my anger. To give me the patience to listen to what others have to say before I begin to respond. To help me be confident in the knowledge that You will help me understand the situation and carefully weigh the wisdom You have planted within me. That You will give me the courage to say the right words or to remain silent.

No matter what is happening in my life, Lord, may the only thing I display to others be the inner light You have sparked and continue to nurture within me. Amen.

He who is slow to anger has great understanding, but he
who is hasty of spirit exposes and exalts his folly. A calm
and undisturbed mind and heart are the life and health of
the body, but envy, jealousy, and wrath are like rottenness
of the bones. . . . Wisdom rests [silently] in the mind and
heart of him who has understanding, but that which is in the
inward part of [self-confident] fools is made known.
PROVERBS 14:29–30, 33 AMPC

Day 135

Lavish Love

Father, You're not holding back on us in Your great love story. You're not worried that we won't return Your affection or hedging Your bets by offering little of Yourself. Instead You've released the dam through Jesus. You've put it all out there.

You've offered *everything* to me—adoption into Your family, a place to belong. You've called me Your child. Not just an acquaintance or a vague friendship, You've folded me into Your family, into Your love. . .You've made me Your daughter. You turn adoring eyes upon me and are delighted when I pull up a chair to Your table. Your Word says that there is no greater love than to lay down one's life for another—and You would know, because You did. Amen.

See what great love the Father has lavished on us, that we should be called children of God! And that is what we are!

1 John 3:1 niv

Day 136

The God of Small Details

Dear God, the depth of Your love is obvious. There is nothing that escapes Your eye. Not one living being goes unnoticed. From me down to the birds, You show care and concern for us all. Every time I begin to worry about the smallest details of my day, remind me that You are the God of small details. Fill me with courage to trust that You see the unmentioned needs buried deep in my pain. Encourage me to share every worry or fear no matter how insignificant they seem to me, knowing they are not insignificant to You. What a gift to be seen and known by the one who created me. In Jesus' name I pray, amen.

Look at the birds in the sky. They do not store food for winter.
They don't plant gardens. They do not sow or reap—and yet,
they are always fed because your heavenly Father feeds them.
And you are even more precious to Him than a beautiful bird.
If He looks after them, of course He will look after you.
MATTHEW 6:26 VOICE

Day 137

Dwelling in Peace

Too many times, Lord, when I look at a situation, I think of all the bad things that could happen. Before I know it, I'm in panic mode, wondering when the things I imagined *could* happen *will* happen. It's enough to drive a girl crazy. But that's not what You would have me do. So I'm coming to You, Lord, to ask You for the strength of Your Son. Help me become the person You created me to be. Give me the encouragement I need to live with others in peace, to see the bright side of life, and to focus on You, the God of love. For when I'm dwelling in peace, You, the God of love and the author of peace, will be with me. In Jesus' name, amen.

Finally, brethren, farewell (rejoice)! Be strengthened (perfected, completed, made what you ought to be); be encouraged and consoled and comforted; be of the same [agreeable] mind one with another; live in peace, and [then] the God of love [Who is the Source of affection, goodwill, love, and benevolence toward men] and the Author and Promoter of peace will be with you.

2 Corinthians 13:11 ampc

Day 138

Rescued

Father, gratitude blooms in my heart each time I consider how You've rescued me and *continue* to rescue me from precarious positions of my own making. Sheep wander aimlessly and fall into dangerous places. Without a shepherd to guide them, they're easily scattered by whatever sight or taste captures their pleasure. And I am no better—easily distracted and often ignoring Your words of warning.

But Father, You *never* give up on me. You have vowed never to leave me or forsake me. You have promised to come and find me in my dark days and pull me from danger. You have accomplished the greatest rescue in the history of mankind by dying for me. Please transform my mess into a message of praise to You. Thank You, Jesus. Amen.

"For this is what the Sovereign LORD says: I myself will search for my sheep and look after them. As a shepherd looks after his scattered flock when he is with them, so will I look after my sheep. I will rescue them from all the places where they were scattered on a day of clouds and darkness."

EZEKIEL 34:11–12 NIV

Day 139

When Worry Subtracts

Dear God, I know that worrying subtracts in my life. It robs and steals from me. It rips away things like peace and harmony. And it leaves a gaping hole in my heart that I can't seem to fill on my own. Looking back, I realize there's never been a time when my worrying accomplished anything good. It has never tweaked the outcome for the better or made me feel stronger in the moment. Instead, anxiety has worked against me. So let this revelation be what drives me to You for help and encouragement every time. Be a powerful and settling force in my life. Restore my peace and hope, and let me find rest in You. In Jesus' name I pray, amen.

*Worrying does not do any good; who here can claim
to add even an hour to his life by worrying?*
MATTHEW 6:27 VOICE

Day 140

Straight Paths

Lord, I've been putting my confidence in the wrong things—my own ideas, insights, and understanding. It's as if I'm trusting my own thoughts over Yours! Yet mine are so flawed and Yours are so perfect. Heaven help me, Lord!

Author of my life, help me to lean on and trust in You and Your Word with all my heart and mind. Help me to remember that *You* hold all wisdom and I don't. Help me, Lord, to acknowledge You every step of my way. Help me to recognize where You are working and to meet You there. Help me to follow Your promptings instead of my own whims. For then I know I will be walking Your way, following Your path. Amen.

Lean on, trust in, and be confident in the Lord with all
your heart and mind and do not rely on your own insight
or understanding. In all your ways know, recognize, and
acknowledge Him, and He will direct and make straight and
plain your paths. Be not wise in your own eyes; reverently fear
and worship the Lord and turn [entirely] away from evil.
PROVERBS 3:5–7 AMPC

Day 141

An Inspiring Influence

Father, thank You for the friends You've gifted to me who make me a better person for having spent time with them. They're encouraging and caring, but they speak with truth from Your Word. They push me to be an improved version of myself.

Truly, my ultimate best friend is You. I am better in every way when I'm with You, Jesus. You gently and lovingly show me where I have been thinking or doing wrong, and You lift me up out of my stress and discouragement. You know everything there is to know about me—You've seen both my obedience and sin—and yet You still love me. Living Your way has brought joy and peace into my days. And I know You will never stop working on me! Amen.

You have stripped off your old sinful nature and all its wicked deeds. Put on your new nature, and be renewed as you learn to know your Creator and become like him.

COLOSSIANS 3:9–10 NLT

Day 142

Speak Hope

Dear God, every time I'm afraid or bogged down by the worries of the day, I'm going to speak hopefulness. I'm going to use my voice to declare Your goodness rather than whimper and crumble under the weight of stress. If I'm scared, I will declare courage. If I'm stressed, I will declare peace. If I'm overwhelmed, I will declare strength. Let the words I say be an encouragement to my soul. I won't stay quiet when my ears need to hear a cheerful and faith-filled word. Help me stay positive. Remind me that I am a victor. And increase my faith to navigate the weary times, knowing You always promise a way out. In Jesus' name I pray, amen.

Worry weighs us down; a cheerful word picks us up.
PROVERBS 12:25 MSG

Day 143

Set Right

Lord, it seems as if the world keeps getting more complicated and difficult. Some days the weight of it drags me down. But then I turn to Your words and my mind is set right.

Thank You, God, for Your loving presence in my life, for accepting me, helping me, taking care of me. Thank You for taking all my worries and woes into Your own hands. My desire is to stick to You like glue. So help me to stay alert, Lord, and to stand firm against the evil in this world. Help me to stay strong in my faith so that I can experience Your precious peace as I live and breathe in Christ. Amen.

Humble yourselves under the mighty power of God, and at the right time he will lift you up in honor. Give all your worries and cares to God, for he cares about you. Stay alert! Watch out for your great enemy, the devil. He prowls around like a roaring lion, looking for someone to devour. Stand firm against him, and be strong in your faith. . . . Peace be with all of you who are in Christ.
1 PETER 5:6–9, 14 NLT

Day 144

The Truth of Christ

Dear God, the Word says I can have strength for every single thing because Jesus empowers me. It's through Him that I can overcome fear. He is the reason I don't get pulled under by stress and strife. I am ready for anything because of Him. But I don't feel that way right now. In this moment, I'm terrified by the situations I'm facing. I am tired of every day bringing a new set of anxieties. I am feeling rather hopeless that my life can ever change. And if You don't shift that mindset in me, I'm worried I'll be stuck here forever. Please help me stand strong in the truth of Christ. I need Your help. In Jesus' name I pray, amen.

I have strength for all things in Christ Who empowers me [I am ready for anything and equal to anything through Him Who infuses inner strength into me; I am self-sufficient in Christ's sufficiency].
PHILIPPIANS 4:13 AMPC

Day 145

Revive Me

Lord, I was weary, worn thin, and beaten down—exhausted from facing another day of fighting the same old battles. My ragged emotions were running the show. But then I turned to Your Word. And I was reminded that You are my strength when I have none. You are my rest when I am tired. You are my peace when my emotions are battered.

When I come to Your scriptures, You gently lead me to the rest and restoration that I crave. You have refreshed and revived my perspective. I am not defeated, and I am not without hope. Thank You, Father, for providing me with what I need—both spiritually and physically. Teach me how to offer kindness and grace to others when they need refreshment too. Amen.

"I will refresh the weary and satisfy the faint."
JEREMIAH 31:25 NIV

Day 146

Go to God

Dear God, I will absolutely take You up on the offer extended in today's verse. I'm coming to You overwhelmed and weary and tired, and I need the kind of rest only You can provide. I'm done trying to fix things myself because I just make them worse. The world has done me no favor except to fray my nerves. And what I really want is to climb into Your lap and cry. I want Your voice to soothe me and Your peace to overwhelm me. I don't like the way the world has treated me, and I need a break. It's been a tough season on so many levels. Help me find relief and refreshment in Your presence. In Jesus' name I pray, amen.

Come to Me, all you who labor and are heavy-laden
and overburdened, and I will cause you to rest.
[I will ease and relieve and refresh your souls.]
MATTHEW 11:28 AMPC

Day 147

I Give You My Cares

Father, my heart aches for the pain of this world. For the fears that crouch in wait and the anxiety that stalks our minds. For the sickness and pain and utter brokenness I see around me. Your creation cries out for a savior. When Jesus rode into Jerusalem, the people cried out, "Hosanna, save us!"

Father, You feel our hurts. You care for us. Jesus wept for us. He died for us. But the story doesn't stop there. You had an intricate and magnificent plan that has existed in You since before the beginning of time. Jesus rose from that grave. He walked out of that tomb. And He lives! I cast my anxiety on You because You love me. You have a plan. You didn't do what was expected and defeat the Roman government—You did something so much greater. You defeated death. You brought life, and with it. . .hope. Thank You, Jesus. Amen.

Cast all your anxiety on him because he cares for you.
1 PETER 5:7 NIV

Day 148

The Divine Exchange

Dear God, teach me to be unafraid. This world breeds fear because it's cruel and demanding. It overexpects and underdelivers. And it has created a fearful heart in me. Too often, I look to others for comfort. I take my brokenness into the world and ask for solutions. I put all my hope for help and healing into incapable hands—including my own. But the Word says You're gentle and humble. It promises rest for me from the cares and fears of the world. And You'll exchange my heavy burden for a yoke that is easy and light instead. I don't have to be afraid because You promise peace. Anytime I begin looking to the world, bring me back to You. In Jesus' name I pray, amen.

"Put on my yoke, and learn from me. I'm gentle and humble. And you will find rest for yourselves. My yoke is easy to bear, and my burden is light."
MATTHEW 11:29–30 CEB

Day 149

On Your Side

Lord, with You on my side, I can do anything You call me to do, no matter how difficult. With You, I fear no one and nothing. When I need a safe and sure refuge, I know You will be there for me, a secure place for me to run to.

So help me, Lord, to trust You more than anyone or anything else. Help me not to depend on other people. They are fallible, but You are not. You are the perfect and incomparable God of all. It's You I look to as my safe haven, You I trust with all I am and have, You I have complete confidence in. In Jesus' name, amen.

The Lord is on my side; I will not fear. What can man do to me? The Lord is on my side and takes my part, He is among those who help me; therefore shall I see my desire established upon those who hate me. It is better to trust and take refuge in the Lord than to put confidence in man. It is better to trust and take refuge in the Lord than to put confidence in princes.
PSALM 118:6–9 AMPC

Day 150

Bear with Me

God, I'm sorry for internalizing my anxieties. You take such good care of me. You speak truth to me and show me what's right. You never allow me to get away with my sin, because it separates me from You. Yet You are gentle in Your leadership. I see the ways that You bear with me in my weakness. Your patience. Your provision. How could I trust any other more than You, my Father? You've given me family to support me and teach me, Your Word to give me wisdom when I'm confused, Your Spirit so I'm never alone.

Smooth the stress from my mind like an unwelcome wrinkle as I lean on You. Father, help me to show Your patience and willingness to support those who are weak. Amen.

We who are strong ought to bear with the failings
of the weak and not to please ourselves.

ROMANS 15:1 NIV

Day 151

At His Feet

Dear God, I've got nothing left in me. My heart is heavy, and I have no energy to carry on. I'm so afraid that my deepest fears will come true and I won't be able to stop them. My resolve to fight back is gone, and I just want to give up because the weight of my worry is too much to bear. When You tell me to leave all my cares and anxieties at Your feet, can I trust You with them? I want to, but there's a control issue inside me that needs to know for sure. Mature my faith so I can be confident to let go and let You replace those fears with grace and strength. In Jesus' name I pray, amen.

So here's what I've learned through it all:
Leave all your cares and anxieties at the feet of the
Lord, and measureless grace will strengthen you.
PSALM 55:22 TPT

Day 152

Sufficient Grace

Father, I struggle with the stress of guilt—guilt over my mistakes and past choices, and even some of my present ones. It seems I fail more often than I'd like in this battle between right and wrong, sin and righteousness.

I used to hide from You because I didn't want to see a look of disappointment or, worse, anger and condemnation on Your face, Father. But everything has changed now. I came face-to-face with Your grace, and I finally understand that Your plan is not for me to be chained in performance-based Christianity, trying to buy Your favor with good deeds. Your love is already given! Your grace means that my guilt is no more. Jesus lived the righteousness that I could not. Thank You, Jesus. Amen.

But he said to me, "My grace is sufficient for you,
for my power is made perfect in weakness."
2 CORINTHIANS 12:9 NIV

Day 153

Birds of Praise

Some days, Lord, I feel as if I'm living hand to mouth. That makes it hard to stay calm. Yet then I read in Your Word that I'm not to worry about my life, what I'll eat, drink, or wear. Because there is more to life than food, drink, and dress. And we are to trust You for everything!

Your birds are a great reminder that You will provide for Your creatures. For they neither plant nor harvest, yet You give them all they need! And in turn, they physically praise You. For every time a bird lowers its beak to drink water, it then lifts its head to heaven—not only to take in the water but to look up to You! May we, Your children, do the same! Amen.

"Don't worry about your life, what you will eat or what you will drink; or about your body, what you will wear. Isn't life more than food and the body more than clothing? Look at the birds of the sky: They don't sow or reap or gather into barns, yet your heavenly Father feeds them. Aren't you worth more than they?"
MATTHEW 6:25–26 HCSB

Day 154

Trust God with Your Needs

Dear God, it seems that too often I look everywhere else for my needs to be met except to You. When my feelings get hurt, I run to my friends and unpack the situation, looking for comfort through their words. When I'm worried about money, I fret in solitude because I don't want to be judged by others. In those scary seasons of parenting when I feel I'm failing, I turn to food and other unhealthy behaviors. I don't want to live this way anymore because it means I am missing out on the awesome display of Your power to answer every need I may have. So, Lord, today I am choosing to surrender my needs to You. In Jesus' name I pray, amen.

*My God will meet your every need out of his riches
in the glory that is found in Christ Jesus.*
PHILIPPIANS 4:19 CEB

Day 155

Believe

Father, my stress is rising again. Fear is battling for my mind amidst the uncertain circumstances that are taking hold in our world. I must fortify my defenses against the enemy by staying in Your Word daily.

And so. . .I choose belief. I believe in You, God. I believe in Your power and that You oversee everything that goes on in this world. You're never thinking, *Oh, I didn't see that one coming. What am I going to do?* I believe in Your promises to be with me always, to fill my mind with peace, to love me, to provide for my needs. I believe what You have told me, Father, and so I place my full trust in You. And my heart is not troubled by the chaos around me. Amen.

"Don't let your heart be troubled. Believe in God; believe also in me. In my Father's house are many rooms. If it were not so, would I have told you that I am going to prepare a place for you? If I go away and prepare a place for you, I will come again and take you to myself, so that where I am you may be also."

JOHN 14:1–3 CSB

Day 156

When We Need Our Own Moses

Dear God, I'm humbly asking You to bless me with a Moses in my own life. I need someone who will not only encourage me when I'm struggling but also be quick to challenge me to take the next right step in faith when I feel unable. So often I need to be reminded that You're always with me, guiding each step I take. And like Joshua, there are times I need a bold voice to readjust my focus on that truth. I want someone who believes in me and loves You! So, Lord, please bring me a Moses. And even more, give me a willing heart to listen to and accept that person's wisdom. In Jesus' name I pray, amen.

[Moses said to Joshua,] Be strong and brave! You're going to lead these people into the land the Eternal promised their ancestors He'd give them. You'll give it to them, and they'll give it to their descendants. And He will be leading you. He'll be with you, and He'll never fail you or abandon you. So don't be afraid!

DEUTERONOMY 31:7–8 VOICE

Day 157

Like a Shepherd

Lord, when I feel weak, I remember Your strength. When I feel alone, I know You are on Your way. You will remember, rescue, and revive me. No matter who or what comes against me, I know that You hold all the power, You are the champion, You are the victor in every way.

So please come, Lord—come to me now in all Your power. Bless me with Your presence, good shepherd. Nourish me, carry me in Your arms, hold me close to Your heart. Get a tight grip on me and never let me go. For I need Your gentle touch, Your guidance, care, and protection. In Jesus' name, amen.

Messenger of good news, shout from the mountaintops! . . .
Shout, and do not be afraid. Tell the towns of Judah, "Your
God is coming!" Yes, the Sovereign LORD is coming in power.
He will rule with a powerful arm. See, he brings his reward
with him as he comes. He will feed his flock like a shepherd.
He will carry the lambs in his arms, holding them close to his
heart. He will gently lead the mother sheep with their young.
ISAIAH 40:9–11 NLT

Day 158

Solid Ground

Lord, sometimes our emotions can take us on a roller coaster ride. Up. Down. Up and then roaring down again. Excitement can easily spiral into stress and despair when pressure mounts.

But, Father, I know that I don't have to stay on this roller coaster ride of negative emotions, because I know that You can rescue me from being tossed about on a wild ride. You can lift me out of the pit and give me a solid place to stand. You, God, never change. Never falter. Never fail. I put my trust in You. You are the rock where my feet find purchase as You lift me out of a pit of stress and despair. In the name of Jesus, amen.

He lifted me out of the pit of despair, out of the mud and the mire.
He set my feet on solid ground and steadied me as I walked along.
PSALM 40:2 NLT

Day 159

The Call to Encourage One Another

Dear God, I don't have many good friends who encourage me to be strong. Honestly, everyone is battling their own stuff right now. We're all eyeball deep in it. So rather than rely on community for a vote of confidence, I give in to fear and shut down. But God, I want what today's verse reveals. I want friendships where we help one another navigate the tricky situations life brings. There's great value in having someone believe in you—that you have what it takes to get to the other side of the mess. So, Lord, in Your kindness and love, help me find friendships where I can encourage and be encouraged. It'll be a game changer. In Jesus' name I pray, amen.

Each helps the other, each saying to the other, "Take courage!"
ISAIAH 41:6 CEB

Day 160

God Will Vindicate

Dear God, today I choose to hand You my hurt and anger. I'm setting aside my plans for revenge. I'm confessing my battle with fear, and I'm deciding to let go of my tendency to obsess about what offends me. Instead, I'm going to trust that You have seen every injustice that's come my way and will respond to each one at the right time and in Your righteous way. It's not my place to play God, and I confess all the times I have. Thank You for caring about me and knowing those moments when fear fills my heart. Even more, thank You for promising to vindicate me so I don't get tangled in sin as I plot and plan. In Jesus' name I pray, amen.

"All who rage against you will be ashamed and disgraced.
All who contend with you will perish and disappear.
You will look for your enemies in vain; those who
war against you will vanish without a trace!"

Isaiah 41:11–12 TPT

Day 161

Count on God

Dear God, my heart is anxious about so many things right now. I'm battling anxiety on epic levels and just can't seem to find a sustainable sense of peace. I am bogged down by feelings of dread. No doubt this season of life has been extremely difficult, especially with so many things coming at me from every direction. I just feel hopeless, like nothing is going to change. Please hold me tight and let me feel Your presence. Please calm my anxious heart. Be quick to show me the way to peace, and give me courage to walk that path. I can't seem to find my way out of this valley, and I'm counting on You to rescue me. In Jesus' name I pray, amen.

"That's right. Because I, your GOD, have a firm
grip on you and I'm not letting go. I'm telling you,
'Don't panic. I'm right here to help you.'"
ISAIAH 41:13 MSG

Day 162

He'll Carry You

Father, I've carried my children around a lot. It's a pleasure to snuggle them close on my hip and no trouble to hold them. Especially when their little legs just can't keep up or they're feeling a bit defeated by the big world around them. I gather them up into my arms and let them rest while I do the work of keeping up for them.

Father, how comforting to know that You do the same for me. When I am feeling weighed down by the world, You pick me up and carry me through. It's not a strain on You. Help me to remember that my problems are not too big for You; and likewise, there's no care too small or inconsequential to bring to You. Amen.

"And in the wilderness. There you saw how the
Lord your God carried you, as a father carries his son,
all the way you went until you reached this place."

DEUTERONOMY 1:31 NIV

Day 163

Seeing Jesus

No matter how hard things get, Lord, I know that everything will be okay. That's because Your power resides within me. That's why, even though troubles surround me, they won't crush me. Even though I may get confused at times, I won't freak out entirely. And even though others may make things difficult for me because of my faith, I know You will always be with me. When I get knocked down, I am able to rise again. I'm not worried about what others can do to me, because I know what You've already done for me. And that makes every day worth living. For from sunrise to sunset, I have the chance to help others see You through me. In Jesus' name, amen.

Our great power is from God, not from ourselves. We are pressed on every side by troubles, but we are not crushed. We are perplexed, but not driven to despair. We are hunted down, but never abandoned by God. We get knocked down, but we are not destroyed. Through suffering, our bodies continue to share in the death of Jesus so that the life of Jesus may also be seen in our bodies.

2 CORINTHIANS 4:7–10 NLT

Day 164

Miraculous Multiplication

Father, sometimes I worry that there just won't be enough—enough time in the day for all the work that needs to be done; enough money to pay the bills, buy groceries, and pay for those braces my daughter needs; enough energy to care for my family.

Thank You, Jesus, that You have great compassion for us humans who worry about not having enough. Please keep this lesson in my mind: when I give things to You, You are capable of supernatural multiplication, just like You multiplied the fish and bread until every need was met. And You can meet my needs as well. You are my great provider. Please show me where I can be Your hands and provide for someone in need. Amen.

Then he took the seven loaves and the fish, and when he had given thanks, he broke them and gave them to the disciples, and they in turn to the people. They all ate and were satisfied. Afterward the disciples picked up seven basketfuls of broken pieces that were left over.
MATTHEW 15:36–37 NIV

Day 165

Release Control

Dear God, help me release the steering wheel so You can be in the driver's seat of my life. Give me courage to step aside so You have complete freedom to lead and I feel comfortable with following. I realize that having control is my way of attempting to manage the things that scare me. But when I hold on and try to power my way through in my own strength and wisdom, I only end up deeper in stress. Thank You for offering to be my guide through the hard times. Today I happily and officially surrender to Your leading. Give me the courage to trust that You always have my best in mind. In Jesus' name I pray, amen.

Then Jesus went to work on his disciples.
"Anyone who intends to come with me has to let me
lead. You're not in the driver's seat; I am."
MATTHEW 16:24 MSG

Day 166

Embrace Suffering

Dear God, the idea of embracing suffering absolutely terrifies me. What if I stop fighting and it wins? What if it overtakes me and I lose myself? What if I develop a victim mentality and it alienates me from my friends and family? But since Your Word says to embrace suffering, there must be a good reason. Maybe it's because when we fight against something, so often it's in self-defense. It's in our own strength and for self-preservation. If You're asking me to trust You with hard seasons instead, then make me brave. Increase my confidence in Your sovereignty. Teach me how to surrender my will to Yours. And help me shift my perspective so I can trust You over me. In Jesus' name I pray, amen.

"Don't run from suffering; embrace it. Follow me and I'll show you how. Self-help is no help at all. Self-sacrifice is the way, my way, to finding yourself, your true self."
MATTHEW 16:25 MSG

Day 167

Listening Ear

God, increase my faith. May I notice all the ways You have answered my prayers in the past and every little detail You have orchestrated in my life. Like the man told Jesus, "I believe—help my unbelief." Help me to see that You care about every piece of my life.

Father, thank You for watching over me. It soothes my fears to know that You are listening for my prayers. You care about the medical test results I'm anxiously awaiting. You care about my strained relationship with my child. You even care about my misplaced phone. I'm not merely shouting my problems into the cosmos—You pay attention to my life because I'm so very important to You. You listen to my stresses and replace my fears with peace. Amen.

The eyes of the Lord are on the righteous,
and his ears are attentive to their cry.

PSALM 34:15 NIV

Day 168

Remembering Who He Is

I look all around me, Lord, yet I see no hope. Discouraged, I bow my head and pray. And as I pray, I remember who You are, where You are. Amid a bevy of unspoken words, I look up to the mountains, to the sky. And there lie my hope and my help. They come from You, the one who made heaven and earth and me! You won't let me trip up, for You're watching over me. You have a plan and a purpose for all things, including me. And in that assurance, I rest in You, knowing You will keep me safe both now and forever. Amen.

I look up to the mountains—does my help come from there?
My help comes from the LORD, who made heaven and earth!
He will not let you stumble; the one who watches over you will not
slumber. . . . The LORD stands beside you as your protective shade.
The sun will not harm you by day, nor the moon at night. The LORD
keeps you from all harm and watches over your life. The LORD
keeps watch over you as you come and go, both now and forever.
PSALM 121:1–3, 5–8 NLT

Day 169

Look at Jesus

Dear God, help me keep my eyes only on You when I'm afraid. When I'm in scary or uncomfortable situations, keep me from staring at the circumstances that are overwhelming me. I'm tired of living in fear. The reality is I've spent too much time letting my Goliaths knock me off balance in the past. I've given them too much power over my heart. I've entertained them too long in my mind. And the only thing that has done is rob me of joy and peace. I confess these giants have become bigger than You too often. So thank You for Jesus. He is the answer. He's the one who came for freedom. Let me keep my eyes only on Him. In Jesus' name I pray, amen.

*When they opened their eyes and looked around
all they saw was Jesus, only Jesus.*
MATTHEW 17:8 MSG

Day 170

Looking past Charisma

Dear God, I don't want to be easily swayed into believing the wrong things. Sometimes I feel naive and am confused by the charisma of others. Some people can be so persuasive! So please keep me from falling prey to false teachers or ungodly role models. Instead, anchor me in You, Lord. Bolster my confidence in the relationship I have with You so I'm not fearful of falling for the wrong thing. Let me be quick to question something that doesn't sit right in my spirit. Give me Your wisdom and discernment to know the difference between truth and lies. And fill me with courage to stand up for what I know is right. In Jesus' name I pray, amen.

See to it that nobody enslaves you with philosophy and foolish deception, which conform to human traditions and the way the world thinks and acts rather than Christ.

Colossians 2:8 CEB

Day 171

First Place in My Heart

Father, You've told me that only one thing can have first place in my affections. There are no ties for the winner of my heart. And I want to be singularly devoted to You. Yet I worry about money. How can I make more? Will I have enough? Should I be saving more? And how can I spend less?

The worries mount, and stress nibbles at the corners of my peace of mind. But I trust You, Father, to care for me. I don't want the pursuit of money to take first place in my affections. Help me to make wise choices, and give me generosity of heart to serve others with the resources I have. The more I submit my finances to You, the more evident Your provision for me becomes. Amen.

"No one can serve two masters. Either you will hate the one and love the other, or you will be devoted to the one and despise the other. You cannot serve both God and money."
MATTHEW 6:24 NIV

Day 172

Heart's Desires

Sometimes, Lord, it seems as if those who are not Your children get all the breaks, money, and success they want. And those of us who are following You, working to do good and to love others, get the short end of the stick. But then I come to Your Word, and I'm reminded that those who do wrong will not live forever in You. They will go the way of all those who have no interest in You. No matter what rewards they may get on earth, I know mine are awaiting me in heaven. So while I'm here, I'll trust in You and do what You created me to do. I'll delight in Your trustworthy presence, depending on You for all I need. Then, even here, You will give me what my heart desires. In Jesus' name, amen.

Don't worry about the wicked or envy those who do wrong.
For like grass, they soon fade away. Like spring flowers,
they soon wither. Trust in the LORD and do good.
Then you will live safely in the land and prosper. Take delight
in the LORD, and he will give you your heart's desires.
PSALM 37:1–4 NLT

Day 173

Path Finder

Lord, the world questions Your power when You don't just step in and fix all the situations in this life that go haywire. They want to know whether You're really out there or just a myth or fantasy figment of our imagination. . .or if You have no will or strength to change things here on earth.

But I know there are things I can't see—things I don't yet understand. But You do, and I trust in You with my whole heart. I will not rely on what little sense I can make of confusing situations but rest my mind on Your great love for me. Give me wisdom and direction in this broken world. I know You have laid out the best path for me. Amen.

Trust in the LORD with all your heart; do not depend on your own understanding. Seek his will in all you do, and he will show you which path to take.
PROVERBS 3:5–6 NLT

Day 174

Advocate

Dear God, give me courage to be bold in my advocacy of others. Help me stand strong for those who feel too weak to stand for themselves. Help me speak for those who are afraid, whose voices have been silenced. What we think and feel matters! Would You give me eyes to see the vulnerable and help me meet them with compassion? Fill my heart with love for the needy and poor. I don't want to be afraid to advocate when it's necessary. I don't want to be afraid to be Your hands and feet in the world. Strengthen me to defend anyone You put on my heart. And give me confidence in You that can't be shaken by insecurity. In Jesus' name I pray, amen.

Speak out on behalf of the voiceless, and for the rights of all who are vulnerable. Speak out in order to judge with righteousness and to defend the needy and the poor.
PROVERBS 31:8–9 CEB

Day 175

Good Enough

Dear God, I have such a fear of never being good enough. It's something that's been with me for as far back as I can remember. So many people have reiterated it through the years that I've adopted it as truth. Wrapping my brain around the fact that You fully accept me is hard to do. Knowing You've folded me into Your family is a powerful revelation I'm trying to grab on to. Believing I will never be alone or abandoned feels foreign. But, Father, I want all these truths to be settled in my spirit. I want them to be alive in me. And I don't want the fear of falling short to have any room to grow anymore. In Jesus' name I pray, amen.

And you did not receive the "spirit of religious duty," leading you back into the fear of never being good enough. But you have received the "Spirit of full acceptance," enfolding you into the family of God. And you will never feel orphaned, for as he rises up within us, our spirits join him in saying the words of tender affection, "Beloved Father!"

ROMANS 8:15 TPT

Day 176

A Way Out

Lord, I know You don't set Your laws because You are a kill-joy, a hater of fun, or an overbearing dictator. You set up boundaries to protect me. . .because You love me. And just as dangerous things happen when a river floods and spills over its banks onto the land around it, dangerous and heartbreaking things happen when I ignore the boundaries You have placed around my life.

Father, show me where I am ignoring Your guidelines, and give me strength to resist the urge to do things that are outside of Your law—and not because I think that my good behavior will gain me heavenly brownie points. I want to obey because I love You with my whole heart for all the ways You love me so completely. Amen.

The temptations in your life are no different from what others experience. And God is faithful. He will not allow the temptation to be more than you can stand. When you are tempted, he will show you a way out so that you can endure.
1 Corinthians 10:13 NLT

Day 177

My Bubble of Predictability

Dear God, stepping out of my comfort zone is terrifying. I like the safety of my bubble of predictability because I'm in control there. So the idea of changing things and doing something new feels out of control. I don't like it. But Your Word says that no matter where I go, You are with me. It says You will watch over me and stay close always. Would You increase my faith so I can have steadfast confidence in these promises? I want to live in faith, trusting You for my next step. And if that means I step out of the bubble and into something new, give me the courage to follow where You lead. In Jesus' name I pray, amen.

Know I am with you, and I will watch over you no matter where you go. One day I will bring you back to this land. I will not leave you until I have done all I have promised you.
GENESIS 28:15 VOICE

Day 178

Transformed

Lord, sometimes when things seem off-kilter in my life, I have to stop in my tracks and look in the mirror. That's when I realize I'm slipping, looking to be a woman who copies the styles and fads of this world instead of the woman *You* want me to be, the woman You *created* me to be. A woman of Christ.

So here I am before You, Lord. Help me to stop looking to the world as my guide. Transform me into a new woman, *Your* woman, by changing the way I think. For then I will find that beautiful woman You created me to be, the one who worships You and is transformed in You. In Jesus' name, amen.

I plead with you to give your bodies to God because of all he has done for you. Let them be a living and holy sacrifice—the kind he will find acceptable. This is truly the way to worship him. Don't copy the behavior and customs of this world, but let God transform you into a new person by changing the way you think. Then you will learn to know God's will for you, which is good and pleasing and perfect.

ROMANS 12:1–2 NLT

Day 179

Sheltered by His Wings

Dear Father, I'm having one of those days where I just want to crawl back into bed and cover my head and hide from the world and my feelings. It all seems so overwhelming, and I feel so weak and worried. Thank You for the ability to hide under Your wings instead; Your strength and reassurance calm my soul in a volatile world.

After just a short time of being nurtured by Your words and truth, I am ready to crawl out from under Your feathers and face the day—strengthened by the promises I believe. I will lean into Your strength. When the winds of worry howl against me, Your faithfulness will spread over me like a broad, impenetrable shield. In Jesus' name, amen.

He will cover you with his feathers, and under his wings you will find refuge; his faithfulness will be your shield and rampart.
PSALM 91:4 NIV

Day 180

Please Be Big

Dear God, sometimes I don't know what to do next. I freeze up in my fear, scared to stand still or make a move. It's confusing and frustrating at the same time. In those times when I feel helpless, please be big. I don't always know how to pray or what to ask for, but You know exactly what to do. I trust that You will intervene at the right time and in the right way. I believe in my heart that You are mighty to save and always have my best in mind. So please help me. Respond to my hopelessness and grow my confidence in Your love and protection. I am looking to You alone. In Jesus' name I pray, amen.

"O dear God, won't you take care of them?
We're helpless before this vandal horde ready to attack
us. We don't know what to do; we're looking to you."
2 CHRONICLES 20:12 MSG

Day 181

In Returning

I need You, Lord. When the day's worries about the present and the night's fears about the future begin to consume me, I come to You. For only by returning to You and resting in You will I be saved from all the fretting and fuming that nags and gnaws at my spirit. I will be strengthened when I lie down, quietly and confidently trusting in You. Happy I am as I wait for You, looking for and longing for Your presence, Your blessing, Your love, Your joy, Your peace, and best of all, Your companionship. What more could a woman ask? In Jesus' name, amen.

Thus said the Lord God, the Holy One of Israel: In returning [to Me] and resting [in Me] you shall be saved; in quietness and in [trusting] confidence shall be your strength. . . . Blessed (happy, fortunate, to be envied) are all those who [earnestly] wait for Him, who expect and look and long for Him [for His victory, His favor, His love, His peace, His joy, and His matchless, unbroken companionship]!
ISAIAH 30:15, 18 AMPC

Day 182

My Soul's Anchor

Lord, I come before You to worship as I am standing in the wake of a storm. As the storm was raging and I was being blown about, I started to lose my bearing. But You have been faithful and steadfast, you have anchored my soul—firm and unmoving. As the winds blew strong and the waters rose, You rescued me and pointed me due north when the horizon was cloaked in darkness.

Thank You, Father, for Your ever-present protection. My hope is in the life that You give—the grace, forgiveness, mercy, love, and abundant, forever life. And this hope steadies me when the climate around me becomes dark and dangerous. I know that my soul and my eternity rest securely with You, Jesus. Amen.

We have this hope as an anchor for the soul, firm and secure. It enters the inner sanctuary behind the curtain.
HEBREWS 6:19 NIV

Day 183

But We Have the Lord

Dear God, help me be fearless because I know You are always with me. In those moments when I want to cower, give me courage. When I feel intimidated, make me brave. When I begin to crumble in my own strength, remind me that You are with me, fighting! Life may look overwhelming from my human perspective. I may feel small in relation to the Goliath in front of me. My situation may threaten and taunt me with hopelessness. But when I put my trust in You, Lord, all the power of heaven is backing me up. Let this be my battle cry as I walk through the ups and downs of life. Let this be why I can stand fearless! In Jesus' name I pray, amen.

"All he has is human strength, but we have the LORD our God, who will help us fight our battles!"
2 CHRONICLES 32:8 CEB

Day 184

He Is Your Friend

Dear God, thank You for being my best friend. Thank You for wanting to be invested in my life in meaningful ways. I'm so grateful that You promise to shepherd my heart as I walk through life. Let these truths sink deep in me, giving me courage and confidence that I can overcome anything that stands in my way. Knowing I'll always have more than enough of whatever it is that I need through Your generosity encourages me to stay strong through the storms of life. I know You will be faithful to equip me. You will defend my heart. You will bless my life. And that means there is no fear that can overtake me. In Jesus' name I pray, amen.

Yahweh is my best friend and my shepherd.
I always have more than enough.

PSALM 23:1 TPT

Day 185

The Solid Rock

Today I praise You, Lord, for all You are to me. You are a solid rock, a stable and immovable pillar for me in an unsteady world. You are the one I can run to for protection and strength. With You within me, I can do anything You've called me to do. You are the one who sets me free, who guides me in the right direction, who puts me on the best path. You make my feet like those of a deer so that I can climb mountains without missing a step. You defend me and raise me up to heights I've never known before. What a wonderful Lord You are! Amen.

Is there any god like GOD? Are we not at bedrock? Is not this the God who armed me well, then aimed me in the right direction? Now I run like a deer; I'm king of the mountain. He shows me how to fight; I can bend a bronze bow! You protect me with salvation-armor; you touch me and I feel ten feet tall. You cleared the ground under me so my footing was firm.
2 SAMUEL 22:32–37 MSG

Day 186

Sure as the Sunrise

God, I come before You both anticipating the great things You will do in my life and the world around me, and simultaneously suffering from doubt that You would show up in my mess as I wait in the cloaking darkness. I'm so tired. And fear slithers into my soul because I can't yet see Your movements in this enfolding blackness. How long, Lord, until You come?

Loving and merciful Father, please forgive my weak faith. I know You will give me strength and courage each day, each hour, and each moment as I need it. Just as the night watchman is convinced of the advancing sunrise, I too am sure that You hear me and will answer. May everything I experience bring glory to Your name. Amen.

I wait for the LORD, my whole being waits, and in his word I put my hope. I wait for the Lord more than watchmen wait for the morning.
PSALM 130:5–6 NIV

Day 187

Finding Rest

Dear God, I'm desperate for rest. The battle has been so intense lately, filling me with all kinds of fear. It has exhausted me because I am always on guard, always hypervigilant of what's going on around me. My heart is full of anxiety, and I'm worried about all sorts of things that could go wrong. What's more, I don't see any relief in sight. Please give me peace. Please soothe my fears as You restore me. I am too weak, Lord, and I'm asking You to straighten the crooked paths I'm on right now. Bring me out of the chaos and help me steady my gaze on You. Fill me with confidence that with You I will always find rest! In Jesus' name I pray, amen.

He provides me rest in rich, green fields beside streams
of refreshing water. He soothes my fears; He makes me
whole again, steering me off worn, hard paths to roads
where truth and righteousness echo His name.
PSALM 23:2–3 VOICE

Day 188

Because You Believe

When worries crowd my mind, Lord, I feel anything but blessed. Thoughts of my troubles tend to leak into my soul and weigh down my spirit. But then I am reminded of Your promise never to leave me. To do the impossible in and through me. To be with me always. To fill me with Your presence. So I ask You, Lord, to tell me today what promise You would have me hold on to in this moment, knowing I will be blessed—blessed because I believe You will actually do all You say You'll do. In Jesus' name, amen.

At the sound of Mary's greeting, Elizabeth's child leaped within her, and Elizabeth was filled with the Holy Spirit. Elizabeth gave a glad cry and exclaimed to Mary, "God has blessed you above all women, and your child is blessed. Why am I so honored, that the mother of my Lord should visit me? When I heard your greeting, the baby in my womb jumped for joy. You are blessed because you believed that the Lord would do what he said."

LUKE 1:41–45 NLT

Day 189

Heaven's Dew

Father, I admit that my life doesn't feel very blessed right now. I'm struggling to see the good through the blinding haze of bad that obscures my vision. Things aren't going my way; in fact, invisible forces seem to be moving circumstances against me.

But, Father, I know that Your blessings for me are still here. And while You may not be blessing me with material things that I wish I had, You have blessed me with Yourself. Your Word says that You are a friend that sticks closer than a brother. And I have experienced Your amazing friendship. I believe that You want to bless me, Father. Please reveal to me any hidden sin that may be hindering Your good blessings for me. And thank You for sticking with me always. Amen.

May God give you heaven's dew and earth's richness.
GENESIS 27:28 NIV

Day 190

Unending Shadows

Dear God, sometimes it seems I'm disappearing into the unending shadows surrounding me. Right now, I'm fighting to navigate what feels like darkness in some of the relationships that mean the most to me. I'm worried about losing people I love, scared they may walk away from me. I feel like I can't do anything right in their eyes, and it seems we're always at odds. It's this instability that scares me because I don't want to lose them. Please put a hedge of protection around me. Guide me into truth and show me the next step. You are a good God, and I trust You to shine a light so the unending shadows are no longer an issue. In Jesus' name I pray, amen.

Even in the unending shadows of death's darkness, I am not overcome by fear. Because You are with me in those dark moments, near with Your protection and guidance, I am comforted.
PSALM 23:4 VOICE

Day 191

You Are Pursued

Dear God, I love knowing You pursue me now and always will. It calms my heart to realize there's nothing I can do to make You walk away from me. I can't sin too much. I'll never run out of second chances with You. And there's a hope-filled future waiting for me. So when I begin to project negativity about how tomorrow may look, remind me that Your heart for me is good. Whisper into my spirit that Your love never fails. Breathe joy and peace into my soul, giving me courage to stay the course in faith. And never let me forget that once my race on earth is done, I will spend forever in Your glorious presence. In Jesus' name I pray, amen.

So why would I fear the future? Only goodness and tender love pursue me all the days of my life. Then afterward, when my life is through, I'll return to your glorious presence to be forever with you!
PSALM 23:6 TPT

Day 192

He Understands

Father, I've been lonely. My emotions cry out that no one understands what's going on in my life. My family doesn't get the stress I'm under, and I feel as if there's no one I can talk to. But I know that You are with me always. And that You *do* understand, regardless of how I feel.

Jesus, You walked this lonely earth. You were misunderstood, mocked, abused, beaten, betrayed, and killed. You cried real tears in this world. You understand me completely and fully, because You walked a more treacherous road than the one I tread. I ask You to take my troubles and replace them with Your peace. I don't want to carry this load of baggage anymore. Thank You, Jesus, for listening, for understanding, for saving me. Amen.

Pile your troubles on GOD's shoulders—he'll carry your load,
he'll help you out. He'll never let good people topple into ruin.
PSALM 55:22 MSG

Day 193

God Listens to You

Dear God, please hear what's on my heart. Even when the words don't come out right, or don't come out at all, hear me. Know the intimate details of every fear that has me tangled in knots. See the heaviness of thought that's on my mind right now. Feel the weighty insecurities that are keeping me from standing up for myself. And understand the reasons I am paralyzed and unable to make decisions. I'm a mess and desperate for the sweet relief only You can bring. I simply cannot take the next step because I lack courage. My confidence is shot, and I'm not sure of my next move. Please help me, Lord. I'm waiting. In Jesus' name I pray, amen.

I am passionately in love with God because he listens to me.
He hears my prayers and answers them. As long as I live I'll keep
praying to him, for he stoops down to listen to my heart's cry.
PSALM 116:1–2 TPT

Day 194

Compassion

I want to be like You, Lord. When You heard the sad news about Your cousin John the Baptist, You stepped away for a bit by Yourself. Yet when others came to be blessed or healed by You and followed You, You had compassion on them and healed them.

Help me, Lord, to be as selfless as You. Make me a woman who has the capacity to put her own troubles aside and help those in need. Give me that kind of heart, that kind of energy, that kind of empathy, that kind of desire. Fill me with Your spirit of kindness and compassion so that I may serve You as You served others. Amen.

He [King Herod] sent and had John beheaded in the prison. . . . Now when Jesus heard this, he withdrew from there in a boat to a desolate place by himself. But when the crowds heard it, they followed him on foot from the towns. When he went ashore he saw a great crowd, and he had compassion on them and healed their sick.

MATTHEW 14:10, 13–14 ESV

Day 195

Bursting Hope

Father, I have to keep the bigger picture in mind when I'm feeling overwhelmed with life. I was a sinner destined for eternal death before I met Jesus. And nothing that I could do myself could save me. I was in a hopeless and dire situation. But Your mercy saved me. You chose to give Your Son in my place so that I can experience life and hope in salvation.

Thank You, Jesus, for Your sacrifice! When life seems too much, I need only to remember that this world is fleeting. My cares and troubles here won't last forever, because Jesus has overcome the world. I have lasting victory no matter the battles I might lose today. My future is one of bursting hope! In Jesus' name, amen.

*He saved us, not because of righteous things we had done,
but because of his mercy. He saved us through the washing
of rebirth and renewal by the Holy Spirit, whom he poured
out on us generously through Jesus Christ our Savior.*
TITUS 3:5–6 NIV

Day 196

Kind and Gracious

Dear God, some of my favorite things about You are the kindness and graciousness You've shown me. Whether I'm dancing high on a mountaintop or dragging myself though a dark valley, You hear me. You see me. And I can remember countless times You've reached down from heaven and saved me. In strength, You doused my fear so it didn't own me. With Your help, worry never consumed me—at least not for long. You made me brave when I felt anything but. I see the value in looking back at Your track record in my life, remembering every single time You showed up. Thank You for those memories. Bring them to mind anytime I need encouragement. In Jesus' name I pray, amen.

I cried out to the Lord, "God, come and save me!" He was
so kind, so gracious to me. Because of his passion toward
me, he made everything right and he restored me.

PSALM 116:4–5 TPT

Day 197

Wholly Leaning

Lord, I realize I do lean on You for some things, handing You my concerns in certain areas. But I have yet to lean my entire self upon You. For some reason, I find myself holding part of me back. So help me, Lord, to trust fully in You. Remind me that because You are my helper, I need not be worried about or afraid of anything.

You, Lord, are the Creator of this universe. You sustain it all. You, the mightiest of all, rule over every people and every big and little thing. So in this moment, in this time and place, I give You all of me, Lord. Today I place myself and my total trust and confidence in You, Your power, Your wisdom, and Your goodness. Amen.

We take comfort and are encouraged and confidently and boldly say, The Lord is my Helper; I will not be seized with alarm. . . . What can man do to me? Remember your leaders and superiors in authority. . . . Imitate their faith (their conviction that God exists and is the Creator and Ruler of all things, the Provider and Bestower of eternal salvation through Christ, and their leaning of the entire human personality on God in absolute trust and confidence in His power, wisdom, and goodness).
HEBREWS 13:6–7 AMPC

Day 198

Ultimate Sacrifice

Father, sometimes I feel unseen. Unnoticed. My suffering doesn't move anyone around me into action. It makes me feel alone. Isn't anyone willing to help me?

I have read in scripture that my help comes from You. My spirits lift as I realize that even if no person aids me or offers comfort, my Good Shepherd already has. It is no trivial thing You have done for me. It is the biggest, the *hardest*, sacrifice anyone could ever make on my behalf and the grandest gesture of love I will ever receive—Jesus, my good shepherd, You laid down Your life for me. It wasn't taken from You. You decided to give it up—for me. In the precious name of my shepherd, Jesus, amen.

"I am the good shepherd. The good shepherd
lays down his life for the sheep."

JOHN 10:11 NIV

Day 199

Power of Praise

Dear God, I know there's power in praise. It has a beautiful way of lightening the heavy load I'm carrying. Recognizing Your greatness builds up unshakable confidence in my spirit. It quickly melts away fear that keeps me stuck, unable to move forward. When I choose to focus on Your goodness instead of my messiness, I feel a surge of hope deep in my heart. Yes, I know I'm deeply loved by You! Help me remember to praise You in the storm as I wait for You to rescue me. When I'm feeling down, move me to count all the ways You have been big in my life. When things feel overwhelming, point me to the Word for unmatched encouragement. In Jesus' name I pray, amen.

Praise GOD, everybody! Applaud GOD, all people! His love has taken over our lives; GOD's faithful ways are eternal. Hallelujah!
PSALM 117:1–2 MSG

Day 200

His Love Never Quits

Dear God, thank You that Your love never quits. I'm grateful that no matter what, You'll never give up on me. In a world where love feels shallow and conditional, what a relief to know Yours never is. And it's Your love that helps me conquer fear. I know the promises packed into the love You offer, and they steady me when life feels overwhelming. I can always go back to You with my heartbreak and fear because Your love never fails to meet me right where I am. I will stand strong because You straighten my back with confidence. And in those times when I forget these things, rush in a reminder so I feel courageous to press on! In Jesus' name I pray, amen.

Thank GOD because he's good, because his love never quits.
Tell the world, Israel, "His love never quits." And you,
clan of Aaron, tell the world, "His love never quits."
And you who fear GOD, join in, "His love never quits."
PSALM 118:1–4 MSG

Day 201

Thirst Quencher

Father, this life has a way of wringing me out, leaving me feeling depleted, parched, dried up. But I praise You that I don't have to wallow in that withered state. I know just where to go—to the well of living water.

Father, Your Holy Spirit fills me up until I am overflowing with Your fruits. I know that You are the only well that will never run dry, my source of forever life. I've tried other things, God—money, success, family—but they aren't enough. They don't fully satisfy this driving thirst for You. I want more of Your Spirit. Revive me with Your living waters. Father, with You I will never need another source to quench this desire inside of me. Amen.

Jesus answered, "Everyone who drinks this water will be thirsty again, but whoever drinks the water I give them will never thirst. Indeed, the water I give them will become in them a spring of water welling up to eternal life."
JOHN 4:13–14 NIV

Day 202

Safe Place

Lord, without You in my life, all is chaos. I have no comfort. Worries drag me down. I do nothing but sigh in consternation. That's why I run to You each and every day. Keep and protect me, Lord. Be my safe place of refuge. Let me catch my breath as I lean into You, trusting You with everything I am and have.

You, Lord, are the best thing in my life. When I feel as if I'm being pulled in ten different directions, I come to You. And You calm me down, give me the peace, comfort, and wisdom I need. Thank You for being with me and taking care of me. Because of You, I have a lovely life. In Jesus' name, amen.

Keep and protect me, O God, for in You I have found refuge,
and in You do I put my trust and hide myself. I say to
the Lord, You are my Lord; I have no good beside or beyond
You. . . . The Lord is my chosen and assigned portion,
my cup; You hold and maintain my lot. The lines have fallen
for me in pleasant places; yes, I have a good heritage.
PSALM 16:1–2, 5–6 AMPC

Day 203

God Is Your Father

Dear God, be my Father right now. Fill the void my earthly father left in my life. Teach me all the things he should have taught me. My heart aches for the father I needed and wanted but didn't get. There are deep wounds and fears he left in my heart—places exposed and unhealed. Please open my eyes to see all the ways You're filling that gap. Let me know You're making up the difference. The pain I've experienced because my earthly father failed me is extensive. But You, Lord, have rescued me without fail. You've been faithful to calm my anxiousness and begin healing my insecurities. And I'm so grateful You are my Father. In Jesus' name I pray, amen.

Out of my deep anguish and pain I prayed, and God, you helped
me as a father. You came to my rescue and broke open the way
into a beautiful and broad place. Now I know, Lord, that you
are for me, and I will never fear what man can do to me.
PSALM 118:5–6 TPT

Day 204

He Never Sleeps

God, I rest securely in the knowledge that there are no surprises for You in my life—or in the vast entirety of Your creation. Your Word promises that You are ever watchful, never sleeping, always vigilant. I can rest in peace knowing that You are guarding my life at all times. Never caught unaware. Never shocked. Never unsure. Never needing to "wait and see."

You know all. You see all. Everything past, present, and future is within Your scope of vision. And knowing this brings the greatest comfort and peace to my life. How can I allow worry to rise within me when the eternal, omnipotent, omniscient God of everything that ever was, is, and ever will be is watching over me? Thank You, God, for Your constant care. Amen.

Indeed, he who watches over Israel will neither slumber nor sleep.

PSALM 121:4 NIV

Day 205

Trusting God over People

Dear God, help me break the lifelong habit of putting my trust in people. Not only do I eventually feel let down or abandoned, but it's not fair to them either. They're not my savior, and thinking they are sets them up for failure. By design, they aren't that powerful. I don't want to continue looking to my friends and family to rescue me. I don't want to tax them with my struggles or come off as too needy. Instead, let me remember to bring my fears and frustrations directly to You because You'll never see me as too much. I won't ever be too needy in Your eyes. My faith is in You. In Jesus' name I pray, amen.

It is better to put your faith in the Eternal for your security than to trust in people. It is better to put your faith in Him for your security than to trust in princes.
PSALM 118:8–9 VOICE

Day 206

No Other God

Whenever the going gets tough, Lord, I need an extra dose of help. From You I need the faith to defy those who force me to do what is against Your will and way. Help me to stand up for myself and stick close to You, knowing that the threats of others are nothing to me because I have You in my life. Remind me that You will be with me whether I am rescued in this world or not. No matter what happens, I will follow and obey You alone. For You are my true and only God, the all-powerful, all-knowing Savior whom I will love and serve in this life and the next.

Shadrach, Meshach, and Abednego replied, "O Nebuchadnezzar, we do not need to defend ourselves before you. If we are thrown into the blazing furnace, the God whom we serve is able to save us. He will rescue us from your power, Your Majesty. But even if he doesn't, we want to make it clear to you, Your Majesty, that we will never serve your gods or worship the gold statue you have set up."

Daniel 3:16–18 NLT

Day 207

A Safe Place

God, I've seen the ruins of ancient castles from dangerous times gone by. Thousands of squat stones laid one upon another to form sturdy, protective walls where the people of the land could take shelter when their enemies attacked.

Father, I need a safe place to hide when my enemy is attacking—a place that has proven itself to be strong and impenetrable. You are that strong place for me, God. I know that You will take care of me because You are faithful. Your Word says that You are a strong tower I can run to when I'm afraid. Shelter me from the enemy's fiery darts. They're finding their marks from all angles today. Strengthen me with Your armor so I can face these spiritual attacks. Amen.

But the Lord is faithful, and he will strengthen
you and protect you from the evil one.
2 THESSALONIANS 3:3 NIV

Day 208

Can't Outlast His Love

Dear God, I know fear isn't stronger than You. It can't outlast or outblast Your love. Anxiety crumbles the moment I bring You into the mix. I can't even count the number of times I've seen this happen in my life. But there are moments when I still forget this truth that I need to know without fail. This information is life changing. Your love has the power to bring healing and hope to the things that threaten to drain every ounce of my courage. Lord, please help me grab on to You every time I feel afraid. I don't want to give in to fear ever again. Instead, I want to bask in Your glory and goodness—forever! In Jesus' name I pray, amen.

So let's keep on giving our thanks to God, for he is so good! His constant, tender love lasts forever!

PSALM 118:29 TPT

Day 209

The True Path

My true path is discovered, Lord, when I look to You for all things. When I seek Your wisdom. When I hear Your voice speaking to my heart at night. That's why I want to keep You, Your Word, and Your Spirit always with me. With You in my midst, nothing can shake me up, bring me down, or turn me around.

I am amazed at the peace that You and Your presence give me, Lord. You make my heart glad. Joy springs from my lips. I burst into songs of praise. For You make me feel as light as a leaf upon the wind. Because of You, I find the rest and safety and clear path I need to live this life for You. Amen.

I will praise the LORD who counsels me—even at night
my conscience instructs me. I keep the LORD in mind always.
Because He is at my right hand, I will not be shaken.
Therefore my heart is glad and my spirit rejoices; my body also rests
securely. . . . You reveal the path of life to me; in Your presence
is abundant joy; in Your right hand are eternal pleasures.
PSALM 16:7–9, 11 HCSB

Day 210

Evidence of Things Not Seen

Father, sometimes it's hard to keep my faith focused on my expectant hope. I get discouraged and stressed out by the reality that is bearing down on me, the hurts I feel, the stress that tenses me, the fears that smother, and I lose sight of where my hope rests.

My hope rests in a coming reality that is as sure as the morning sunrise. I can't see it yet, but I know with certainty that I will spend eternity in a wondrous place with You—a place void of pain, empty of sin, and filled with Your comforting light. I know that I live under Your grace. I know that You love me greatly. I can't see it now with my eyes—I'm living in a world of "not yet"—but my hope is securely fastened to this fantastic future. Amen.

Faith shows the reality of what we hope for;
it is the evidence of things we cannot see.
HEBREWS 11:1 NLT

Day 211

That Kind of Courage

Dear God, when I read about what Your Son went through to pay for my sin and bridge the gap it left between me and You, I'm in awe. From my human viewpoint, I would have been so afraid to face it. I would have begged for a way out to avoid the pain and humiliation. But He never wavered in the reason He came to earth. Jesus had an eye on His purpose. And if there was any fear to speak of, it never interfered. Give me that kind of courage. Let me approach hard things in that way. Allow my steadfastness to show as I rise up in bravery regardless of what comes my way. In Jesus' name I pray, amen.

He was oppressed and harshly mistreated; still he humbly submitted, refusing to defend himself. He was brought like a gentle lamb to be slaughtered. Like a silent sheep before his shearers, he didn't even open his mouth.

ISAIAH 53:7 TPT

Day 212

Alpha and Omega

Lord, sometimes uncertainty can swipe my feet right off the solid ground I thought I was standing fixedly on. I may not be able to feel certain about how things in my life are going to turn out—I may become ill, I may lose my job, my child may make a huge mistake—but I can be sure of one very important thing: You, God, are never uncertain about how anything is going to end.

You hold the past, present, and future in Your capable hands. You are the beginning of all things and the end. You are the Almighty. Father, give me peace as I bathe my stress-filled mind in the knowledge that You are the Alpha and the Omega. Amen.

"I am the Alpha and the Omega," says the Lord God,
"who is, and who was, and who is to come, the Almighty."
REVELATION 1:8 NIV

Day 213

The Silver Lining

Dear God, it's hard to imagine that my troubles and struggles
have a silver lining. Where I only see them as a mess, You see
the whole picture. They may feel like doom and gloom to me,
but there is great purpose in the trials I face. And when I only
see a Goliath, You already know the outcome of the battle. I
need Your perspective. Let me peek behind the curtain so I
can find the courage to battle on. Help me be fearless as I trust
You in my circumstances. Help me be positive rather than
shrivel up in fear and worry. Help me see the purpose, and
bless me with confidence in You! In Jesus' name I pray, amen.

*I have good news, brothers and sisters; and I want to share
it. Believe it or not, my imprisonment has actually helped
spread the good news to new places and populations.*
PHILIPPIANS 1:12 VOICE

Day 214

Loving Commands

I know Your two commandments, Lord Jesus, the ones that tell me I'm to love the Father with all my heart, soul, and mind and I'm to love my neighbor as myself.

Not once did You say worries will help me inherit eternal life. So help me break the fretting frenzy. Help me to let my worries about the past, present, and future fade away. Wasting my time being consumed by fears, concerns, and anxieties just depletes the energy I need to follow Your loving commands. But to get to that worry-free place, Lord, I need and now request the gift of Your calm, Your peace, and Your presence, in this moment and every moment to come. Amen.

*Just then an expert in the law stood up to test Him,
saying, "Teacher, what must I do to inherit eternal life?"
"What is written in the law?" He asked him. "How do you
read it?" He answered: Love the Lord your God with all your
heart, with all your soul, with all your strength, and with all
your mind; and your neighbor as yourself. "You've answered
correctly," He told him. "Do this and you will live."*
LUKE 10:25–28 HCSB

Day 215

He Fights for You

Lord, whenever I'm feeling anxiety's crushing fist tightening around my chest, help me to remember that this battle is not mine. . .it's Yours. My stress relaxes its choke hold on my life when I realize that it's not up to me to force things to happen. When I am faithful to You, seek Your will, study Your Word, and submit to You, You fight the battle for me.

The Israelites weren't victorious in taking the stronghold city of Jericho because they went out and scaled those intimidating walls and trained day and night with sword and shield; they won because they obeyed Your words to them. . .and then You crushed the walls standing in front of them. Father, please fight this battle for me. Amen.

"This is what the Lord says to you: 'Do not be afraid or discouraged because of this vast army. For the battle is not yours, but God's.'"
2 CHRONICLES 20:15 NIV

Day 216

Inspired by Overcomers

Dear God, there is nothing more encouraging than watching someone stand strong during tough seasons of life. It gives me strength for what's ahead and helps me feel hopeful that everything will be okay. When I want to give in and bury my head in the sand, remembering the testimony of an overcomer spurs me on. Lord, let me be that for others. Let my story be what inspires someone else to stay positive and hopeful. Keep me focused on Your goodness every time fear threatens to steal my peace. Whether I'm scared because of a diagnosis, a bill, an argument, or something else, with Your help I can be fearless and resolved. In Jesus' name I pray, amen.

Not only that, but most of the followers of Jesus here have become far more sure of themselves in the faith than ever, speaking out fearlessly about God, about the Messiah.

PHILIPPIANS 1:14 MSG

Day 217

A Prayer Habit

I want to have a powerful prayer life like Daniel, Lord. No matter what, he stayed committed to You and so was supported and protected by You. Because Daniel bowed down to You, kneeling in prayer before You, this faithful follower was able to rise above his trials and those trying to bring him down.

So help me, Lord, to get into my own prayer habit. Prompt me to meet You at the same time and place every day. To be committed to doing so. Then I too, as I bow down to You, will be able to rise above whatever comes my way. Amen.

The administrators and high officers went to the king and said,
". . .Give orders that. . .any person who prays to anyone, divine
or human—except to you, Your Majesty—will be thrown into the
den of lions. . ." So King Darius signed the law. But when Daniel
learned that the law had been signed, he went home and knelt
down as usual in his upstairs room. . . . He prayed three times
a day, just as he had always done, giving thanks to his God.
DANIEL 6:6–7, 9–10 NLT

Day 218

Focus on the Father

Father, I feel exhausted by the frenzy of activity that is my life. I'm always in a hurry, constantly weighing what things I have room for in my day.

Please help me to prioritize my time in a way that glorifies You. I feel less stressed when I pause my day to spend time with the most important friend I have. I'm stopping the mad rush right now to still my rampant thoughts and restless body and think about what it means to my existence that You are God. You hold me together when I'm losing it. You bring peace to my panic. Calm to my crazy. Faith to my fear. Thank You for being all that I am not. In the name of Jesus, amen.

He says, "Be still, and know that I am God; I will be exalted among the nations, I will be exalted in the earth."

PSALM 46:10 NIV

Day 219

Victory for Good Reason

Dear God, the victory through You over my debilitating fear matters for lots of reasons. It puts the spotlight on Your awesomeness and might. It points to endless possibilities as I trust in You. And it shows the power of prayer. Even more, my freedom from fear highlights You as a healer. For so long, I tried to figure out my problems on my own. I am capable! But I discovered that my own strength had huge limitations, and I wasn't able to be my own savior for long. I couldn't squash the fear that had a tight grip on me. But You came through for me time and time again. And I give You the glory! In Jesus' name I pray, amen.

"But I've left you standing for this reason: in order to show you my power and in order to make my name known in the whole world."

EXODUS 9:16 CEB

Day 220

The Good Portion

Too often, Lord, I feel like I'm a Martha. I have good intentions at the beginning of the day. I am quiet and focused on You, attending to Your will and way. But then the next thing I know, I'm caught up in a flurry of activity, and whatever sense I had of Your presence has flown out the window! I don't want to live that kind of life, Lord, where my anxieties, concerns, and troubles crowd in on me and crowd You out. Help me, Lord, to choose that good portion, the one where I sit at Your feet, undistracted and captured by Your words and presence. Amen.

Mary. . .seated herself at the Lord's feet and was listening to His teaching. But Martha [overly occupied and too busy] was distracted with much serving; and she. . .said, Lord, is it nothing to You that my sister has left me to serve alone? . . . The Lord replied. . .Martha, Martha, you are anxious and troubled about many things; there is need of only one or but a few things. Mary has chosen the good portion. . .which shall not be taken away from her.
LUKE 10:39–42 AMPC

Day 221

No Hiding Places

God, Your Word is full of people who tried to hide from You. Jonah ran off in a boat, Adam and Eve snuck off to the bushes, and Elijah hightailed it to a cave. And I too have done my share of trying to keep things from You.

I'm not sure why any of us thought hiding would work. I know that Your presence fills the entire universe. There's nowhere I can go that You can't find me. And yet, when I don't want to face You with my sin, my fear, my disobedience, I try to run the other way. But I know that no action of mine could ever separate me from Your love. Your grace covers even my worst moments. Thank You, Jesus, for finding me. Amen.

"Who can hide in secret places so that I cannot see them?" declares the LORD. "Do not I fill heaven and earth?" declares the LORD.
JEREMIAH 23:24 NIV

Day 222

The Challenge of Good Courage

Dear God, I know Your desire is for me to respond with courage at every turn. I know that when it feels impossible to be brave, I can find bravery through You. And I understand how important it is for others to see a healthy level of confidence from me because it helps them feel confident too. But there are times I just want to hide instead. Sometimes it just feels too overwhelming and I've lost my gumption to fight on. It's in those times I am desperate for hope. This is when I need others to come alongside me with reassurance and encouragement. This is when I need You to intervene with supernatural strength and confidence. In Jesus' name I pray, amen.

*Be of good courage and let us behave ourselves
courageously for our people and for the cities of our God;
and may the Lord do what is good in His sight.*
1 CHRONICLES 19:13 AMPC

Day 223

Warrior versus Worrier

Lord, no matter what happens in my life, help me to trust in You completely. Help me to walk with You so closely, to serve You so faithfully, that not one bump in the road, not one word of discouragement, not one setback, not one sign of trouble will keep me from following wherever You lead, from doing whatever You would have me do, from serving whenever You want me to serve. Give me the strength of heart to be a woman warrior, not a fretful female. For my heart's desire is to live a life of confidence, not cowardice. In Jesus' name I pray, amen.

A stone was brought and placed over the mouth of the den. . . . Very early the next morning, the king got up. . . . "Daniel, servant of the living God! Was your God, whom you serve so faithfully, able to rescue you from the lions?" Daniel answered, ". . .My God sent his angel to shut the lions' mouths so that they would not hurt me." . . . Not a scratch was found on him, for he had trusted in his God.
DANIEL 6:17, 19–23 NLT

Day 224

Share the Love

Father, I wonder sometimes if I'm getting this Christian walk thing wrong. Am I doing what You would have me do? Am I missing Your voice? Leaving opportunities on the table? My life feels, well. . .small. Despite my devotion to You, is my little life really that meaningful in Your kingdom?

But then I read Galatians, and I realize that You really did make it very simple. I need to love others—in big ways, in small ways, in easy ways, and sometimes in hard ways. It's not complicated calculus or mysterious deception. You want me to live my life loving others as You have loved me. . .to go around doing good works so that others will be drawn to the light of Your goodness. Show me who needs a little love today. Amen.

For the entire law is fulfilled in keeping this one command: "Love your neighbor as yourself."

GALATIANS 5:14 NIV

Day 225

All the Glory

Dear God, thank You for being my rescuer and protector. So often, I come to You with all my fears and troubles. And while I know that's okay, right now I just want to recognize the awesomeness of who You are. I want to acknowledge all the ways You've blessed me over the years. I want to give every bit of the glory to You for the faithfulness that's been shown to me. Your trustworthiness has healed some places in me where I've experienced betrayal and abandonment from others. And when my fear has taken hold of me, You have been my rescuing knight every single time. Today God, all the glory is Yours. I love You. In Jesus' name I pray, amen.

Blessed be GOD, my mountain, who trains me to fight fair and well. He's the bedrock on which I stand, the castle in which I live, my rescuing knight, the high crag where I run for dear life, while he lays my enemies low.
PSALM 144:1–2 MSG

Day 226

Sitting by the Roadside

Sometimes I find myself sitting on the sidelines, wondering how I will ever get rid of all that plagues me. I wonder when I will see the solution to my problems or have enough to see me through more than a day. And then I realize You, Lord Jesus, are so very near. Although I cannot see You, I feel Your presence. That's when I begin to shout out for You! I ask for Your love, compassion, and mercy. I ignore the tumult around me, focusing on You alone. Lord, I beg You, help me! Free me from my cares and concerns as I seek to draw ever closer to You. Amen.

Bartimaeus, a blind beggar, a son of Timaeus, was sitting by the roadside. And when he heard that it was Jesus of Nazareth, he began to shout, saying, Jesus, Son of David, have pity and mercy on me [now]! And many severely censured and reproved him, telling him to keep still, but he kept on shouting out all the more, You Son of David, have pity and mercy on me [now]!

MARK 10:46–48 AMPC

Day 227

He Opens Minds

Heavenly Father, my heart is burdened for my loved ones who do not see You. I want to pester them and get on my soapbox and preach about Your love and grace. I want to provide the key that unlocks their chains and releases them from their tormentors.

But my burden is lifted when I remember that You alone have the key to open their eyes and to give them ears to hear. It is my role not to be their Holy Spirit but to be a reflection of Your love and a witness to Your resurrection through the peace and grace You have given me, as I continually pray for those dear to my heart. Draw them close to You, Lord, and open their minds to understand. Amen.

Then he opened their minds so they could understand the Scriptures. He told them, "This is what is written: The Messiah will suffer and rise from the dead on the third day, and repentance for the forgiveness of sins will be preached in his name to all nations, beginning at Jerusalem. You are witnesses of these things."
LUKE 24:45–48 NIV

Day 228

A Fierce Protector

Dear God, can I be honest? I'm asking You to vindicate me in big ways—visible ways. I need You to storm out of heaven on my behalf and fight for me. I'm too afraid to battle on my own because I'm unskilled, but You are my protector. And I'm asking You to be fierce. Can You see me down here cowering in fear, drowning in the ocean of hate that's pulling me under? Please save me. Please pull me from this scary situation and instill courage in my heart. Let me witness You battling all that's come against me. It will do my heart so good to see justice and mercy lean in my direction. In Jesus' name I pray, amen.

Step down out of heaven, GOD; ignite volcanoes in the hearts of the mountains. Hurl your lightnings in every direction; shoot your arrows this way and that. Reach all the way from sky to sea: pull me out of the ocean of hate, out of the grip of those barbarians who lie through their teeth, who shake your hand then knife you in the back.

PSALM 144:5–8 MSG

Day 229

Spiritual Eyesight

Thank You, Lord, for stopping for me, for calling me. Seeking Your presence, I take up my courage and I throw off everything—troubles, pride, worries, sins—that might hinder my running to You. When I reach Your side, You ask me, "What do you want Me to do for you?" And my answer is clear and true. "Lord, let me see You. Open my spiritual eyes to You, Your ways, and Your truth."

Then I hear You say, "Go your way; your faith has healed you." And at once I can see You. Not wanting to leave Your side, I follow You down the road, never to part from You. Amen.

Jesus stopped and said, Call him. And they called the blind man, telling him, Take courage! Get up! He is calling you. And throwing off his outer garment, he leaped up and came to Jesus. And Jesus said to him, What do you want Me to do for you? And the blind man said to Him, Master, let me receive my sight. And Jesus said to him, Go your way; your faith has healed you. And at once he received his sight and accompanied Jesus on the road.
MARK 10:49–52 AMPC

Day 230

Change a Single Life

God, what could I possibly do to impact the brokenness, pain, and hopelessness of this world? I'm only one person, and I'm not a particularly rich or impressive one at that. I live a normal life, and yet I feel an underlying anxiety over the depressing state of our world and the pain I see on faces around me.

But I realize after reading this scripture from Hebrews that I can share. I can lift a burden—even if it helps only a single person. And tomorrow I can help another. You're so pleased with my sacrifice of doing good in this hurting world. Today I will worship You by chatting for a while with my lonely, elderly neighbor. The feelings of helplessness are lifting from my heart already. Thank You, Jesus. Amen.

Make sure you don't take things for granted and go slack in working for the common good; share what you have with others. God takes particular pleasure in acts of worship—a different kind of "sacrifice"—that take place in kitchen and workplace and on the streets.
HEBREWS 13:16 MSG

Day 231

Bible Blessing

Dear God, let today's scripture be a blessing for me. With all that I've endured in this season, I'm asking You to make this my reality. These past few months have been so heavy. I'm feeling overwhelmed with all that life has been throwing my way. Lord, I need a break. My biggest fear is that nothing will change. I'm terrified my current situation will be forever. And I just don't have the strength to go on. I can't continue this way any longer, exhausted from the battle and angry that I feel stuck. Rescue me and restore me to a bountiful life full of examples of Your goodness. Let me breathe fresh air in Your presence. In Jesus' name I pray, amen.

Our barns will be filled to the brim, overflowing with the fruits of our harvest. Our fields will be full of sheep and cattle, too many to count, and our livestock will not miscarry their young. Our enemies will not invade our land, and there'll be no breach in our walls.

PSALM 144:13–14 TPT

Day 232

The Right Path

When I don't know the right way to go, I turn to You, O Lord. For Your knowledge and wisdom are deep. You can see the way that lies before me. You know where I've come from, the trials and troubles I've endured.

So, dear Lord, lead me by Your truth. Teach me all I need to know so that I can rest, stop, or turn to the right or left, wherever You bid me go—or not go. I'm looking for a fresh outpouring of the love You've always held for me, Lord. Rain it down upon me now so that I will find the strength and energy and wisdom to do as You will.

Show me the right path, O LORD; point out the road for me to follow. Lead me by your truth and teach me, for you are the God who saves me. All day long I put my hope in you. Remember, O LORD, your compassion and unfailing love, which you have shown from long ages past. Do not remember the rebellious sins of my youth. Remember me in the light of your unfailing love, for you are merciful, O LORD.

PSALM 25:4–7 NLT

Day 233

Righteousness by Faith

Father, sometimes I wonder what You're up to. Your ways
don't always make sense to me. I'm in awe of Noah. He lived
in a desert, cocooned in heated sunshine. And You told him
to build a giant boat because a flood was coming. Noah had
no evidence of this impending disaster except His faith in
Your words. And he worked tirelessly for years, much to the
mocking delight of his neighbors, to build that boat. He was
obedient despite whatever he may have thought about the
probability of a flood.

I wonder, in the midst of Your warnings, do I laugh and
keep right on doing what I've been doing? Or do I believe with
all my heart and obey You. Father, help me leave this gnawing
doubt and selfishness to follow You wholeheartedly. Give me
faith like Noah! Amen.

*It was by faith that Noah built a large boat to save his family from
the flood. He obeyed God, who warned him about things that had
never happened before. By his faith Noah condemned the rest of
the world, and he received the righteousness that comes by faith.*

HEBREWS 11:7 NLT

Day 234

Everything and Everyone

Dear God, when I'm feeling afraid and worried about life, remind me that You are in complete control. The whole world is in Your capable hands, so there is nothing I should fear. Nothing is bigger than You. So let that powerful fact give me the courage I need to believe I am covered by You, especially when I feel scared. Let it be what reinforces my confidence that nothing escapes Your gaze—not even for a moment. Let it support my deepest hope that good things will happen and truth will always prevail. For You are the judge who presides over everything and everyone. And because I am Yours, I'm in good hands. In Jesus' name I pray, amen.

All rise! For God now takes his place as judge of all the earth. Don't you know that everything and everyone belongs to him? The nations will be sifted in his hands!

PSALM 82:8 TPT

Day 235

Sharpen Me

Father, I've felt a prickling unease slide up my spine when I'm with certain people. Some are negative, critical, and doubtful about everything and everyone they encounter. I've also realized that others' gossip loosens my lips too—and before I know it, I'm discussing my friends' private lives and handing down judgments I've no business making. I find myself sliding into ungodly behavior when I spend time with these people.

Father, please forgive me for not keeping my guard up against gossip and criticism. Help me to gently limit my time with those who don't encourage me to behave in a godly way and to be intentional in shining for You when I'm with them. Send me a friend who will sharpen me to live better. And help me to be a friend like this to others. Amen.

As iron sharpens iron, so one person sharpens another.
PROVERBS 27:17 NIV

Day 236

Shake, Shake, Shake

Dear God, rather than let my fears shake me, let my prayers shake heaven and earth! Let me pray with such power and strength that it destabilizes the things trying to weaken me. Let me be quick to bring my worries directly to You, full of hope and expectation for relief. I know the world can be scary. It's full of people and situations that threaten my resolve to trust You. And while I'll face moments when I feel weak, the Holy Spirit makes me strong! I am fortified though my belief in You, Lord. Continue building my faith so I can stand in courage and confidence even when my life feels knocked off balance. In Jesus' name I pray, amen.

They finished their prayer, and immediately the whole place where they had gathered began to shake. All the disciples were filled with the Holy Spirit, and they began speaking God's message with courageous confidence.

ACTS 4:31 VOICE

Day 237

Bold and Believing Faith

You know who I am, Lord. You know the struggles I've had, the challenges I have overcome. My concern is that I seem to believe more in my own powers than Yours. In other words, I need a faith lift.

Help me, Lord, to rely on You, have faith in You, and trust in You. Give me the boldness to follow You, shouting out that I need Your mercy, Your compassion, Your support. Help me to see that You are the answer to all my questions, the source of all I need. And when You ask me if I believe You can help me, may I say, "Yes, Lord, yes!" For I know that because of my faith, what I desire will be provided. Amen.

Two blind men followed along behind him, shouting, "Son of David, have mercy on us!" They went right into the house where he was staying, and Jesus asked them, "Do you believe I can make you see?" "Yes, Lord," they told him, "we do." Then he touched their eyes and said, "Because of your faith, it will happen." Then their eyes were opened, and they could see!
MATTHEW 9:27–30 NLT

Day 238

Content No Matter What

Lord, I like peaceful décor, comfortable furniture, and luxurious rugs. I enjoy being surrounded by beautiful treasures I've found. And sometimes I see something that costs more than I should spend, but my mind stays a bit obsessed with how much I want it. I try to replace it with a different thought or remind myself that I don't need it, but I keep picturing it decorating my space. And too often I give in and buy it.

Father, teach me contentment. And not just with my things but in difficult circumstances too. Hard times come, and I just want an escape. But You sustain me, Father. You fill up the emptiness of my dissatisfaction. Help me to be truly content, no matter what. In Jesus' name, amen.

I don't have a sense of needing anything personally. I've learned by now to be quite content whatever my circumstances. I'm just as happy with little as with much, with much as with little. I've found the recipe for being happy whether full or hungry, hands full or hands empty. Whatever I have, wherever I am, I can make it through anything in the One who makes me who I am.

PHILIPPIANS 4:11–13 MSG

Day 239

Where You Step

Dear God, would I be more courageous if I knew without a doubt that everything would work out? If I knew my steps were always numbered and covered by Your favor, might I be more intrepid? If I knew I couldn't fail, would I be braver? Regardless, help me trust where You lead. Give me timely reminders that, no matter what, You're with me. You aren't looking for perfection. Instead, You're looking for a willing heart to follow You. Make my heart willing. Mature my faith. Show me how to walk audaciously. And make me gutsy enough to step out of my comfort zone as I choose to trust and follow You. In Jesus' name I pray, amen.

"I am giving you every place where you set foot, exactly as I promised Moses. . . . No one will be able to stand up against you during your lifetime. I will be with you in the same way I was with Moses. I won't desert you or leave you."

Joshua 1:3, 5 CEB

Day 240

A Friend Indeed

Here I stand before You, Lord, waiting for a good word to fall from Your lips and into my ear. I'm waiting for You, Lord, to give me the direction I need, to tell me the words that will soothe my soul and give me hope. For You, Lord God, are my comforter, friend, beloved, helper, counselor, and refuge. My eyes are constantly on You, for You hold all wisdom and power. You are the one who rescues me from evil. So look upon me now, Lord; see how deeply distressed I am in heart and spirit. Save me from all my problems and lift me to Your place of peace.

Who are those who fear the LORD? He will show them the path they should choose. They will live in prosperity, and their children will inherit the land. The LORD is a friend to those who fear him. He teaches them his covenant. My eyes are always on the LORD, for he rescues me from the traps of my enemies. Turn to me and have mercy, for I am alone and in deep distress. My problems go from bad to worse. Oh, save me from them all!

PSALM 25:12–17 NLT

Day 241

On Guard

God, why do I so easily forget that I'm living in a battle zone? Spiritual forces are at war in this world, and souls are on the line. Eternity hangs in the balance for some, and I need to fight. Help me to see anxiety and stress as weapons of the enemy. He wants to see fear wash white across my face and doubt spill darkness in my eyes when I come up against him.

Father, keep me vigilant in watching for his attacks, and help me stand firm in faith. When fear mounts, I know You will be my courage. Give me wisdom in recognizing sin and temptation for the lethal attacks against Your kingdom that they are. Gird me with strength as I face this day. I rest in Your inexhaustible power. Amen.

Be alert, stand firm in the faith, be courageous, be strong.
1 Corinthians 16:13 csb

Day 242

Maybe It's You

Dear God, it's hard to imagine that I may be part of the solution. I've never considered myself a leader because it felt too risky—too scary. For so long, I've sat back and let others take the lead. But I'm beginning to feel courage in my spirit. I'm starting to feel confident in my skills and abilities. Lord, if You're asking me to step into a leadership role, please make it crystal clear. Give me bravery to leave my comfort zone and engage in a new way. Provide me with clarity and vision for the next step. Put hope in my heart. I want to follow You and make a difference, so I say yes! In Jesus' name I pray, amen.

"Be brave and strong, because you are the one who will help this people take possession of the land, which I pledged to give to their ancestors."
JOSHUA 1:6 CEB

Day 243

Like Sheep

Father God, I have found that being a Christian is definitely not a walk in the park—but it's still so much better than any other path. Besides, it is the only path that is right and true! Yet here You are, sending me out like a sheep in the midst of wolves. Still, I won't worry, for when fear begins to creep in, You, the good shepherd, have promised to be right here with me. No matter what happens, I don't need to be anxious or worried, terrified or distressed. I don't even need to worry about what to say when I'm questioned, for Your Spirit will speak through me. What more could a little ewe ask?

I am sending you out like sheep in the midst of wolves. . . . Be on guard against men [whose way or nature is to act in opposition to God]. . . . When they deliver you up, do not be anxious about how or what you are to speak; for what you are to say will be given you in that very hour and moment, for it is not you who are speaking, but the Spirit of your Father speaking through you.
MATTHEW 10:16–17, 19–20 AMPC

Day 244

Hold Me Up

Father, as a child in need of help, I ran to my mom or dad to dry my tears and soothe my scraped-up knees or bruised emotions. And I knew that when I brought my pain to my parents, they wouldn't turn me away. Instead they would be moved by love to wrap me in a hug and take my little fingers to lead me through whatever problem had shoved me down. I rested in the comfort of security as I was cradled in the loving guidance of my parents.

Father, sometimes as a grown-up, I try to be too self-sufficient. I forget who to turn to with my stressed-out anxiety over the problems I have. Father, You alone promise to hold me up. May I never forget to run to You. Amen.

Don't be afraid, for I am with you. Don't be discouraged,
for I am your God. I will strengthen you and help you.
I will hold you up with my victorious right hand.

Isaiah 41:10 nlt

Day 245

The Gift of Remembering

Dear God, I know the value of remembering promises You've spoken to me. It's in the scary moments when I want to quit that the importance of clinging to truth becomes clear. Thinking through all the ways You've shown up to save, heal, and restore in the past will be what bolsters my courage to stand strong in real time. Give me the mind to recall Your faithfulness when I need it the most. Fill my heart with the reality that You've always proved Yourself trustworthy. Keep the enemy from blocking my ability to recall hard proof of Your goodness in my life. I want to remember—I need to remember—because it strengthens me like nothing else can. In Jesus' name I pray, amen.

He said, "Remember what Moses the servant of GOD commanded you: GOD, your God, gives you rest and he gives you this land."
JOSHUA 1:13 MSG

Day 246

The Shepherd Who Carries You

When I am weak, Lord, You are my strength. When I am too fragile to protect myself, You are my shield. In You alone my heart trusts. On You alone I rely. Because I cannot do all things in my own power, I clamor for Your help. Because You are my all in all, I cannot help but sing songs of rejoicing, praising You. For You are the one who saves me from all snares, and even from myself! Yes, Lord, You are my perfect peace.

Thank You, my strength and shield, for blessing and preserving me; for continually nourishing me; for being the shepherd who carries me, in this life and the next. Amen.

The Lord is my Strength and my [impenetrable] Shield;
my heart trusts in, relies on, and confidently leans on Him,
and I am helped; therefore my heart greatly rejoices, and with
my song will I praise Him. The Lord is their [unyielding]
Strength, and He is the Stronghold of salvation to [me]
His anointed. Save Your people and bless Your heritage;
nourish and shepherd them and carry them forever.
PSALM 28:7–9 AMPC

Day 247

Perfectly Peaceful

Lord Jesus, Peter stepped out of a boat to stand on water because he saw You and what was possible through Your power. And he did it! He stood on the waves beside You. Yes, he looked away and began to sink, but what a miraculous example of the amazing things that are possible when our minds are fixed on only You.

If I can focus my thoughts on Your Word and resist the distractions of my stress-filled emotions, if my trust in You can be steadfast and never wavering, You will keep me in perfect peace—even in the middle of an uncertain, hectic, scary life. I trust You, God. I trust Your goodness and strength. I trust Your love and mercy. Keep my thoughts locked on You. Amen.

*You will keep in perfect peace all who trust in
you, all whose thoughts are fixed on you!*
ISAIAH 26:3 NLT

Day 248

Not Caring What Others Think

Dear God, help me stop caring about what others think. I'm tired of giving it dominion over me. Why do I care what they think? All it does is hurt me, leaving me to feel ugly, unlovable, and unwanted. Why do I give others that kind of power over what I think about myself? Why do I fear their judgment? Lord, give me the boldness to focus only on what You think. When those insecurities pop up, let it drive me to Your Word, where I will find encouragement. It's where I'll discover who I am in You. And it will embolden me to live in freedom, trusting that my sense of value is nonnegotiable. In Jesus' name I pray, amen.

"Listen, my beloved friends, don't fear those who may want to take your life but can do nothing more. It's true that they may kill your body, but they have no power over your soul."
LUKE 12:4 TPT

Day 249

Relief and Refreshment

Lord, when I am tired and weary of carrying my burdens upon my own back, finally realizing how much I have picked up along the way, I come to You. For You will give me the rest I need. You will relieve and refresh my soul.

Teach me, Lord Jesus, what You would have me know. Show me what You would have me see. Then I will find the peace and quiet You promise to those who come to You and comfort themselves in You. Then I will find the "unforced rhythms of [Your] grace" (Matthew 11:29 MSG). In Your name I pray, amen.

Come to Me, all you who labor and are heavy-laden and overburdened, and I will cause you to rest. [I will ease and relieve and refresh your souls.] Take My yoke upon you and learn of Me, for I am gentle (meek) and humble (lowly) in heart, and you will find rest (relief and ease and refreshment and recreation and blessed quiet) for your souls. For My yoke is wholesome (useful, good— not harsh, hard, sharp, or pressing, but comfortable, gracious, and pleasant), and My burden is light and easy to be borne.
MATTHEW 11:28–30 AMPC

Day 250

Seek His Wisdom

Father, how often have I wondered and worried about what to do, which choice was the right one? Or if a path even exists that leads through my knotted mess. I've fretted and wrung my hands and probably gained more than a few gray hairs agonizing over what I should say or do—or not do. And all that anxious energy I've expended wearing out my floorboards at midnight is a complete waste. I spark no insight from the deaf walls huddled around me.

All I need to do is ask You. You won't criticize or reprimand me for my questions. Instead, You will give Your advice generously. Father, I need Your wisdom. Show me what to do. In Jesus' name, amen.

If you call out for insight and cry aloud for understanding,
and if you look for it as for silver and search for it as for
hidden treasure, then you will understand the fear of the LORD
and find the knowledge of God. For the LORD gives wisdom;
from his mouth come knowledge and understanding.
PROVERBS 2:3–6 NIV

Day 251

He Never Hides from You

Dear God, in those lonely moments, remind me that You aren't hiding from me. Sometimes I cry out and You feel so far away. I look for evidence of You working in my circumstances, but I can't see it. I crave to experience Your presence and peace, but it eludes me. And this is why I begin to lose hope. My fear multiplies in the loneliness, and I'm overwhelmed. There is nothing better than You to soothe an anxious heart. Only You can calm me when I'm scared and alone. Give me the eyes and ears to know You are always with me. You've promised never to leave or forsake me, and that powerful truth never fails. In Jesus' name I pray, amen.

"You will look for Me intently, and you will find Me."
JEREMIAH 29:13 VOICE

Day 252

The Steps of a Good Woman

Lord, I am so thankful that You have promised to walk with me every step of the way. That You will actually direct my path because I am Your child and am committed to do good in Your name. Even if I trip up, if I make a mistake or take a misstep, I won't be down forever. For You will be right there beside me. You, like any good parent, will grab my hand, lift me up, and set me back on my feet. Thank You, Lord, for all You have done and promise to continue to do in, through, and for me. Amen.

For such as are blessed of God shall [in the end] inherit the earth.
. . . The steps of a [good] man are directed and established by the
Lord when He delights in his way [and He busies Himself with
his every step]. Though he falls, he shall not be utterly cast down,
for the Lord grasps his hand in support and upholds him. . . .
Depart from evil and do good; and you will dwell forever [securely].

PSALM 37:22–24, 27 AMPC

Day 253

All That Glitters

Lord, it seems incredible that the people of Israel, whom You led out of slavery in Egypt through impressive and powerful miracles, could abandon You to worship something cast in gold—utterly powerless, a creation of their own hands. But, Father, I know that sometimes things that glitter catch my attention and distract me from You as well. And when my focus is absorbed into meaningless things, it's no longer centered on You. And when my thoughts stray from You, it's easy to start making poor choices, just like the Israelites did.

Father, keep me from idols—glittery things that have no power in this life. Show me where I've made something more important than You. Keep my mind focused on You, the living and powerful God. Amen.

Then Aaron took the gold, melted it down, and molded it into the shape of a calf. When the people saw it, they exclaimed, "O Israel, these are the gods who brought you out of the land of Egypt!"
EXODUS 32:4 NLT

Day 254

Guts and Grit

Dear God, I want the kind of guts and grit that Joseph of Arimathea showed when he asked Pilate for Jesus' body. I cannot imagine the fear that coursed through his veins as he mustered courage to approach the Roman governor. But he did, and I admire his valor! Let me dig deep and find that same level of nerve. With Your help, let me be bold as I advocate for myself and others. And let me be known as a fearless woman who stands firmly in her faith, an example to encourage the next generation to have courage. Not only is it freeing, but having unwavering confidence will allow me to make a difference in the world. In Jesus' name I pray, amen.

Late in the afternoon, since it was the Day of Preparation
(that is, Sabbath eve), Joseph of Arimathea, a highly respected
member of the Jewish Council, came. He was one who lived
expectantly, on the lookout for the kingdom of God.
Working up his courage, he went to Pilate and asked for Jesus' body.
MARK 15:42–43 MSG

Day 255

Stop Doing, Just Be

I am strung so tightly, Lord. I have been running around like a madwoman, trying to meet all my deadlines, perform all my duties, do all that is expected of me. But this busyness, this idea of being a superwoman who feels she has to do it all, is definitely taking a toll on me. So I come to You, Lord Jesus, in response to Your invitation. I'm ready to come away with You, alone, to a deserted place, and rest. For I cannot and am not made to keep up this kind of pace. I'm ready to get into a boat with You and sail away to a remote spot where I can stop doing and just be with You alone. Amen.

The apostles [sent out as missionaries] came back and gathered together to Jesus, and told Him all that they had done and taught. And He said to them, [As for you] come away by yourselves to a deserted place, and rest a while—for many were [continually] coming and going, and they had not even leisure enough to eat. And they went away in a boat to a solitary place by themselves.
MARK 6:30–32 AMPC

Day 256

Close By

Heavenly Father, my spirit feels crushed under the pressures and cares of this world. My daily worries stifle me, and they seem only to be growing more suffocating. Am I going to lose my job? Are my kids doing well enough in school? How do I care for my elderly parents while I'm raising my kids? What am I going to do without health insurance if someone in my family gets sick? The stress presses in from all sides.

Father, instead of indulging in a panic attack, I choose to spend time in Your Word. And a peace eases the crushing force of worry. You promise that You are close to me when my heart is broken and that You will save me when my spirit is under attack. Thank You, Jesus, for Your saving power. Amen.

The LORD is close to the brokenhearted and
saves those who are crushed in spirit.

PSALM 34:18 NIV

Day 257

Make Me Brave

Dear God, Esther was one gutsy girl. Knowing she could lose her life for exposing Haman's plan and asking the king to save her people didn't cause her to cower in fear. Instead, this queen's bravery sets a beautiful example for how I want to live. She was a risk-taker. She put the needs of others before hers as she chose to stand up for a very worthy cause. She was relentless in pursing the calling on her life, even if it put her in peril. She was fearless. I don't feel strong right now, and I'm asking You to strengthen my faith so I can be a force to be reckoned with. Grow my confidence in You. Make me brave! In Jesus' name I pray, amen.

Queen Esther answered, "If I please the king, and if the king wishes, give me my life—that's my wish—and the lives of my people too. That's my desire. We have been sold— I and my people—to be wiped out, killed, and destroyed."

ESTHER 7:3–4 CEB

Day 258

Strength and Peace

You, Lord, have such strength. Even Your voice can do tremendous things—break cedars, flash lightning, make the woods tremble, strip forests bare. What power! What a thunderous noise You must make!

The blessing here is that You will give me, Your follower, Your lamb, strength to do what You have called me to do, to be what You have already designed me to be. The strength You give will be unyielding and impenetrable. And You will also bless me with the peace I crave. Sign me up, Lord! For with You walking beside me and filling me with such amazing strength, I can kiss my worries goodbye! Amen.

Ascribe to the Lord, O sons of the mighty, ascribe to the Lord glory and strength. Give to the Lord the glory due to His name; worship the Lord in the beauty of holiness or in holy array. . . . The voice of the Lord is powerful; the voice of the Lord is full of majesty. . . . The Lord [still] sits as King [and] forever! The Lord will give [unyielding and impenetrable] strength to His people; the Lord will bless His people with peace.
PSALM 29:1–2, 4, 10–11 AMPC

Day 259

The Gift of Peace

Lord, I live by faith and not by fear. The enemy tries to scare me with things I cannot control, but I choose faith over fear. You have given me a peace that I cannot always comprehend. And the peace I have from You is a gift this world cannot understand.

When others are running around in hysteria because of a crisis, I am filled with peace. When others have no hope in a tragic loss, Your peace washes in like the tide. No insurance policy, government assurance, or amount of money in the bank can imbue me with the saturating peace of mind that comes from knowing You, Jesus. Thank You for giving me peace, and help me to remain faithful in all circumstances. Amen.

I am leaving you with a gift—peace of mind and heart. And the peace I give is a gift the world cannot give. So don't be troubled or afraid.

JOHN 14:27 NLT

Day 260

Expectant and Confident

Dear God, I want to know without any doubt that You are working in my situation. I don't want to cross my fingers and hope. I don't want to waste my time wringing my hands in worry. I want to be full of confidence, assured that You're with me working out every mess I find myself in. I'm not alone! That's a gift You promised to every believer. And it gives me freedom to live with an expectant heart as well as informs how I approach every day. Let me be excited to see how You make a way. Let me be hopeful while I wait for it. And let me reject any fear that tries to take my joy away! In Jesus' name I pray, amen.

Look among the nations and watch! Be astonished
and stare because something is happening in your
days that you wouldn't believe even if told.

HABAKKUK 1:5 CEB

Day 261

Come Ahead!

I don't know what gets into me, Lord, but sometimes I fail to have complete faith in You. I'm eager enough to get out of my comfort zone. But then once I take that first step of faith, I start looking around, wondering, *Who am I to be walking on water?* And that's when the trouble starts—for I've taken my eyes off You.

So help me, Lord, to ignore the wind and waves, or whatever is threatening to sink me. Help me to cling to You, no matter where I am or what I'm doing, knowing that after You have called me, You won't let me drown but will support my walk with You in every way You can.

> *Jesus was quick to comfort them. "Courage, it's me. Don't be afraid." Peter, suddenly bold, said, "Master, if it's really you, call me to come to you on the water." He said, "Come ahead." Jumping out of the boat, Peter walked on the water to Jesus. But when he looked down at the waves churning beneath his feet, he lost his nerve and started to sink. He cried, "Master, save me!" Jesus didn't hesitate. He reached down and grabbed his hand.*
> MATTHEW 14:27–31 MSG

Day 262

Do-Gooder

Father, sometimes my mounting anxiety and stress come from living a life that is too self-focused. Forgive me for getting too distracted by my own needs and forgetting the needs and hurts of those around me.

Remind me today that You have a job for me to do—kingdom work that You have prepared especially for me. Show me today what work You have for me to do. Whether it's picking up groceries for my neighbor or watching a friend's kids, give me a nudge when I see a job that You've prepared for me. And, Father, as I extend my focus beyond myself, my perspective is often corrected, and I see my life for the blessing that it is. As a result, my stress is spiritually relieved. Amen.

For we are his workmanship, created in Christ Jesus for good works, which God prepared ahead of time for us to do.

EPHESIANS 2:10 CSB

Day 263

Powerful Advertising for Faith

Dear God, help me be humble so I recognize that I cannot navigate this life without You. Keep me from puffing up my chest with pride, boasting in my own strength and might as the reason I survived. The truth is I'm unable to thrive without You. I may be an educated and capable woman, but I am limited by the human condition. You are the one to calm the fears that beat me down. You suppress the insecurities telling me I'm not good enough. Your peace is what allows me to keep a healthy perspective in hard times. And when I am quick to give You the credit, it's powerful advertising for faith. In Jesus' name I pray, amen.

Yet we don't see ourselves as capable enough to do anything in our own strength, for our true competence flows from God's empowering presence.
2 CORINTHIANS 3:5 TPT

Day 264

From Mourning to Merriment

Sometimes I get a little arrogant, Lord. I begin to brag about how I've got it made. The next thing I know, I've wandered away from You and disaster falls upon me. So, Lord God, I call out to You. I ask You to lift me above the worries, troubles, and cares of this world. To pull me back into Your sphere, Your Word, Your way.

Then, as suddenly as I call out, "Save me, Lord!" You change my loud wails into victory songs. You change my black dress of mourning into a gown of gladness. Soon I can't help but sing my song of thanksgiving to You, my Lord and Redeemer. Amen.

When things were going great I crowed, "I've got it made.
I'm GOD's favorite. He made me king of the mountain."
Then you looked the other way and I fell to pieces. I called
out to you, GOD. . . . "Help me out of this!" You did it: you
changed wild lament into whirling dance; you ripped off my black
mourning band and decked me with wildflowers. I'm about to
burst with song. . . . GOD, my God, I can't thank you enough.
PSALM 30:6–8, 10–12 MSG

Day 265

Self-Care

Heavenly Father, am I neglecting or mistreating this body, this temple, You've given me? My stress levels have been high, and I know I haven't been taking care of what I've been blessed with. You are not a cruel taskmaster who demands I work around the clock with no relief. You want me to experience rest.

It's been said that sometimes the holiest thing you can do is take a nap. I am run down and in need of physical rest so that I can help others. Father, help me to eat healthy foods, exercise, and sleep so I'm not too exhausted to shine as a light in this world. Thank You, Jesus, for the price You paid for me. I'm going to take better care of Your temple. Amen.

Don't you realize that your body is the temple of the Holy Spirit, who lives in you and was given to you by God? You do not belong to yourself, for God bought you with a high price. So you must honor God with your body.
1 CORINTHIANS 6:19–20 NLT

Day 266

Confidence before God

Dear God, sometimes I'm nervous to talk to You because I'm so aware of how wretched I can be. I'm afraid that You are disappointed in me or angry because of things I've done. I worry that I'm annoying when I ask for the same things over and over again. I'm concerned You may be frustrated because I still haven't figured it out. So the idea of being confident in prayer feels foreign. Please take that feeling from me. I don't want there to be anything that blocks my relationship with You. Instead, I want to believe without a doubt that my sins are forgiven and that Your love for me is unshakable. Help me replace any fear with steadfast faith. In Jesus' name I pray, amen.

And, beloved, if our consciences (our hearts) do not accuse us [if they do not make us feel guilty and condemn us], we have confidence (complete assurance and boldness) before God.

1 JOHN 3:21 AMPC

Day 267

Leap of Faith

There are times, Lord, when I step out in faith and suddenly
find myself between a rock and a hard place, filled with fear.
I begin thinking, *I was safer not stepping out! Why did I ever take this
leap of faith in the first place?* Yet that's when You want me to have
even *more* faith.

So tell me those words I long to hear, Lord. That all I
need to do is take courage, stand still, and watch You work a
miracle. That You will fight for me. That I'm simply to hold
my peace and remain calm. For You are with me. Amen.

*The Israelites were exceedingly frightened. . . . They said to Moses,
. . . It would have been better for us to serve the Egyptians than
to die in the wilderness. Moses told the people, Fear not; stand
still (firm, confident, undismayed) and see the salvation of the
Lord which He will work for you today. For the Egyptians you
have seen today you shall never see again. The Lord will fight
for you, and you shall hold your peace and remain at rest.*
EXODUS 14:10–14 AMPC

Day 268

Working for the Master

Lord, I get grumpy sometimes, and I don't feel like doing things for other people. The enemy whispers, *What have they ever done for you; It isn't fair for you to have to do this; Your boss expects too much of you; Your family doesn't appreciate your sacrifice.* But, Lord, I know that these self-pitying thoughts are not from You.

My stress melts away when I use every moment of my day to worship You. Every job I do—whether it's a big project at work or washing the dishes after dinner—is an act of worship to You. I will work willingly and dedicate every task to bringing You glory through a happy heart of worship. May others see my attitude and be drawn to Your light. Amen.

Whatever you do, work at it with all your heart,
as working for the Lord, not for human masters.
COLOSSIANS 3:23 NIV

Day 269

Wisdom from Others

Dear God, help me find a community of people who are willing to share their stories with each other. It's such an encouragement to hear from others how they made it through a difficult situation. It helps grow my courage to know others survived stormy seasons of life. And it deepens my faith to hear them recount all the ways You intervened on their behalf. I need those truths to anchor me during my own storms. Too often, I've held on to my own ways of thinking. I've depended on my own strength, hoping it would help me power through. But no more. Open my heart to new friendships, and help me fearlessly embrace them. In Jesus' name I pray, amen.

If you think you know it all, you're a fool for sure;
real survivors learn wisdom from others.
PROVERBS 28:26 MSG

Day 270

Before and Behind

There are so many things I love about You, Lord. And one of them is how You look after me. How You always go before me to check out what lies ahead. At the same time, You've got my back by serving as a shield behind me. *And* You walk beside me, live within me, and sit above me. You are everywhere all the time. And not just for me but for all my loved ones. Thank You, Lord, for standing between me and the darkness. Thank You, Lord, for being all the light I will ever need. In Jesus' name, amen.

And the Angel of God Who went before the host of Israel moved and went behind them; and the pillar of the cloud went from before them and stood behind them, coming between the host of Egypt and the host of Israel. It was a cloud and darkness to the Egyptians, but it gave light by night to the Israelites; and the one host did not come near the other all night.

EXODUS 14:19–20 AMPC

Day 271

Pure Light

Father, I don't always understand the things that happen in this world. It would be very easy, when I'm hurting or I see someone who is suffering, to question Your goodness, Your motives, Your ability to control the situation. But instead I choose to trust You despite the heartbreaking results of sin I see around me.

You promise that You are light and only light. You aren't streaked with darkness or hiding ulterior, selfish motives. You are light—bright, piercing, clean light. And there is absolutely no darkness in You. I may not be able to understand the intricate, eternal plan in all its vast details, but I can trust in Your unadulterated goodness and love for me. Amen.

This is the message we have heard from him and declare to you:
God is light, and there is absolutely no darkness in him.
1 JOHN 1:5 CSB

Day 272

The King over Everything

Dear God, help me keep my worldly support in perspective. I know You gave me amazing family and friends and use them in beautiful ways to walk me through tough times. But I also know that You are my source, plain and simple. Your name is above all names. And when I'm battling fear and worry and anxiety, my first stop should be prayer. Give me a healthy view of my community and the role each person is to play in my life, and help me keep my eyes on You first and foremost. They are my earthly warriors full of might, but You are the King over everything! Let me never invert the two. In Jesus' name I pray, amen.

See those people polishing their chariots, and those others
grooming their horses? But we're making garlands for
GOD our God. The chariots will rust, those horses pull
up lame —and we'll be on our feet, standing tall.

PSALM 20:7–8 MSG

Day 273

Friends for Troubled Times

Father, I've been down and feeling stressed and anxious lately. But I choose to stop and thank You right now for the loyal friends You've given me to walk alongside me through this life. They love me no matter what and always direct me to Your Word when I'm saying or doing things that aren't pleasing to You. And when I'm having a rough time or my car breaks down or I lose my job or my child is sick or I'm sick—they lend a hand to help me get through. My friends are truly Your hands and feet in the church. And my family includes some of my closest friends, Jesus. Thank You for sending me help in the form of amazing friends. Amen.

A friend loves at all times, and a brother
is born for a time of adversity.
PROVERBS 17:17 NIV

Day 274

Thank You!

Dear God, too often I forget to thank You for all You've done. Let me remedy that right now. I've been delivered from debilitating fear in places I never thought possible. I have found victory from anxiety over certain issues that have plagued me for years. I'm more confident now than I've ever been, and I'm certain of Your hand in that. I'm learning to be bold as I advocate for my needs and speak up for others struggling to say what's on their mind. I feel strong in my resolve to trust You as we battle the giants in front of me. And I owe every bit of this to Your promise of faithfulness. Thank You! In Jesus' name I pray, amen.

May Yahweh give you every desire of your heart and carry out your every plan as you go to battle. When you succeed, we will celebrate and shout for joy. Flags will fly when victory is yours! Yes, God will answer your prayers, and we will praise him!

PSALM 20:4–5 TPT

Day 275

A Constant, Ready Retreat

Lord, You are such a wonderful example to me. I want to be sure to follow in Your footsteps, to imitate how You lived, breathed, and moved through this world.

I've read how people who needed healing would form a crowd and press against You. How they kept coming after You, hoping for even the slightest touch of Your hand or Your hem.

Please show me, Lord, how to make sure that I, Your servant, have a continually ready retreat. A place where I can go for rest—physically, mentally, spiritually, emotionally. A place where no one can reach me. A place where I can find the peace I need to replenish my energy. Amen.

A vast multitude, hearing all the many things that He was doing, came to Him. And He told His disciples to have a little boat in [constant] readiness for Him because of the crowd, lest they press hard upon Him and crush Him. For He had healed so many that all who had distressing bodily diseases kept falling upon Him and pressing upon Him in order that they might touch Him.

MARK 3:8–10 AMPC

Day 276

He Loved Me First

Father, I'm worn out. I've been working so hard to get into Your good graces, to make You pleased with me. And then I read Your Word and a realization crashes over me, bathing my stress-beaten mind in peace. . . .

You loved me first! I can't work my way into Your affections. And I don't have to! You have *always* loved me. Fully. Completely. Deeply. Unconditionally. Eternally. Your love is so great that Jesus took a harsh punishment that was meant for me. He absorbed Your wrath so that now when You look at me, You see only the pristine, shining righteousness of Jesus. How foolish of me to think that I could add to the work of the cross. Your perfect love drives away all my fears. Amen.

Such love has no fear, because perfect love expels all
fear. If we are afraid, it is for fear of punishment,
and this shows that we have not fully experienced his perfect
love. We love each other because he loved us first.
1 JOHN 4:18–19 NLT

Day 277

Unstoppable

Dear God, sometimes I end up in a negative mindset. Whether I'm overwhelmed by the mess I'm in or I'm starting to fear what I'm facing, my attitude plummets. It hits rock bottom. But I realize it's because I've taken my eyes off You. I've stopped trusting that You see exactly what's happening and are already in the mix, working things out for my benefit and Your glory. So that I'm not a Negative Nelly, refresh my heart to have faith in You. My enemy will not prevail when I choose to believe Your promises to save and protect. In Your name, I can rise up in courage and face fierce enemies with confidence. With You, I'm unstoppable. In Jesus' name I pray, amen.

Our enemies will not prevail; they will only collapse and perish in defeat while we will rise up, full of courage.

PSALM 20:8 TPT

Day 278

Empowered

Father, thank You that I don't have to do this Christian life on my own! I've tried, and I've failed miserably to do the right thing. My spirit is willing, but my flesh is oh so weak.

But I will not let my anxiety over my failures stomp me into the mud. I have a supernatural power source: Your Holy Spirit lives in me. I can hardly comprehend that the same power that created the universe, the same magnificent power that both drives hurricanes and stills storms with a word—the fullness of God's mighty power—lives in me in the form of Your Spirit. All I need to do is ask for Your help. You give me the strength to overcome. And even when I fall, Your grace catches me. Amen.

But you will receive power when the Holy Spirit comes on you.

ACTS 1:8 NIV

Day 279

Courage to Embrace Today

Dear God, give me courage to embrace whatever today brings. Remove any fear that keeps me from being present with those I love. Help me focus on the good things happening right now so I don't wander down the path of despair. I'm not able to predict the future, so I need to stop trying. Instead, fill me with peace in knowing that You see what's coming and are already working things out for my benefit and Your glory. Mature my faith so I can relax as I trust You with anything the future holds. I may not know what comes next, but I know the one who does. He loves me without fail, and that's enough for me. In Jesus' name I pray, amen.

The reality is you have no idea where your life will take you tomorrow. You are like a mist that appears one moment and then vanishes another.

JAMES 4:14 VOICE

Day 280

An Angel before You

There are so many different ways You amaze me, Lord. You have thought of everything to help me get through this life on earth and ultimately to heaven with You. You have sent an angel to go before me and protect me as I journey. And that same angel will lead me safely to the place You have prepared for me. All I need to do is listen and obey. If I do, then You will oppose all those who oppose me! So many blessings in one pronouncement! So many ways You have made sure I will safely reach my end goal—an eternal life of peace with You, the God of all creation who loves me unendingly. My Lord, I thank You. Amen.

"See, I am sending an angel before you to protect you on your journey and lead you safely to the place I have prepared for you. Pay close attention to him, and obey his instructions. Do not rebel against him, for he is my representative, and he will not forgive your rebellion. But if you are careful to obey him, following all my instructions, then I will. . .oppose those who oppose you."

EXODUS 23:20–22 NLT

Day 281

Deep Well of Strength

Heavenly Father, I'm exhausted. The weight of care and worry hang heavy on my body. My emotions are wrung out like yesterday's dishrag. My heart is tired, and I feel empty inside. I'm not sure I have anything left to give. I've been trying to give from my own well. And I realize that I'm scraping out the last of my reserves like a hungry child digging at an empty peanut butter jar.

Father, I need to tap into Your strength reserves. Your power is unlimited, and I'm asking You to revitalize me. Through You I can give and not grow weary. I can serve and not become faint. I'm going to rest my care-worn heart in the hope I have that You've got this, God. Amen.

But those who hope in the LORD will renew their strength.
They will soar on wings like eagles; they will run and
not grow weary, they will walk and not be faint.

ISAIAH 40:31 NIV

Day 282

Your Tomorrows

Dear God, I can't sit in the fear of tomorrow any longer. It keeps me up at night, robbing me of much-needed sleep. It steals my joy throughout the day as the stress creeps in unexpectedly. It makes me project terrible outcomes down the road that leave me feeling completely hopeless. For my heart's sake, I need to leave these fears and anxieties at Your feet and trust You to handle every one of them. I'm just so overwhelmed with dread for what the future may hold and tired of fighting the onslaught of negatives. Give me the strength to let go of control and let You take the wheel. You are the better driver anyway. In Jesus' name I pray, amen.

Instead you should say, "Our tomorrows are in the Lord's hands and if he is willing we will live life to its fullest and do this or that."
JAMES 4:15 TPT

Day 283

Meeting with the Lord

On days when peace seems elusive, I reach out to You, dear Lord. I want to meet with You, speak with You, feel Your presence. I want to see You, know all about You, and have a personal experience with You.

You are my Lord. You are the one I worship, the one I trust to fill the holes in my life. I want You to be my constant companion—my provider, peace, friend, food, shelter, and shield. Dwell in my midst, Lord. Teach me what I need to know. Be here in this moment, reaching out for me as I reach out to You, spirit to Spirit, heart to heart, breath to breath. Amen.

I will meet with you to speak there to you. There I will meet with the Israelites, and the Tent of Meeting shall be sanctified by My glory [the Shekinah, God's visible presence]. . . . And they shall know [from personal experience] that I am the Lord their God, Who brought them forth out of the land of Egypt that I might dwell among them; I am the Lord their God.
EXODUS 29:42–43, 46 AMPC

Day 284

Your Will Be Done

Father, I'm facing something difficult and frightening that I'd much rather not have to endure. I'm asking, as Jesus did, that if You would, please deliver me from the pain. I know that You are a mighty and all-powerful God who is more than capable of moving on my behalf and changing my circumstances in a blink. But, Father, I also know that You are a good and loving God who is working out a plan for my good.

So I trust You, good Father, enough to say, even if You don't remove these circumstances from me, I will still love and praise You. I will still trust You. I will still put my faith and hope in You. Nevertheless, not my will, but Yours, be done. Amen.

> *"Father, if you are willing, take this cup away from me—nevertheless, not my will, but yours, be done."*
>
> LUKE 22:42 CSB

Day 285

Help Others Grow

Dear God, if I'm here to help other believers grow their faith, I need help, because I don't feel like a leader myself. I don't feel responsible enough to influence others. Sometimes I battle debilitating fear as I step out of my comfort zone and trust You when life falls apart. I worry that You're too busy for my issues. And while I know I should be clinging to You for hope, too often I sit in my stress and strife alone. So how can I be a spiritual leader? Help me trust that if You call me to this, it means You will also equip me to walk it out. And make me fearless as I do. In Jesus' name I pray, amen.

Now, those who are mature in their faith can easily be recognized, for they don't live to please themselves but have learned to patiently embrace others in their immaturity. Our goal must be to empower others to do what is right and good for them, and to bring them into spiritual maturity.

ROMANS 15:1–2 TPT

Day 286

Living Hope

Lord, at times life drags me down because I've put my faith in foolish things. Forgive me for searching out something to compensate for my lack of faith in Your ability to handle this situation on my behalf.

But You have given me a new hope. To hope is to trust or believe that something will happen, and I realize that I had placed my hope in worldly things—money, my own abilities, my government, my family. Help me to remember that my hope is rooted in Your great mercy, in the resurrection of Jesus. Because He died and rose again on the third day, I have hope for today and for my eternal future. In the name of Jesus, amen.

Praise be to the God and Father of our Lord Jesus Christ!
In his great mercy he has given us new birth into a living hope
through the resurrection of Jesus Christ from the dead.
1 PETER 1:3 NIV

Day 287

Asking Others to Pray

Dear God, I get so nervous asking others to pray for me. I wish I had the confidence of Paul in today's verse when he boldly asked for help. He didn't show any timidity at all! I end up worried that my requests will be ignored. I worry that someone might think they are silly or trivial. What if I ask for prayer in confidence and then they share it with someone else? It just feels too risky, like a setup to be embarrassed. Lord, You're going to have to bring my heart around on this one. You'll need to make me courageous enough to be vulnerable with others. And I am asking that You do! In Jesus' name I pray, amen.

Brothers and sisters, I urge you, through our Lord Jesus
Christ and through the love of the Spirit, to join me
in my struggles in your prayers to God for me.
ROMANS 15:30 CEB

Day 288

Worker of Miracles

Lord Jesus, You are the worker of miracles. When everyone has given up all hope, You come on the scene, hear our requests, and answer in a power-filled way.

So here I am before You, Lord, with a problem. My trust in You, my belief, may be less than either of us would like. But it is there. And You have promised that even with faith the size of a mere mustard seed, my prayer will be answered. I believe You *can* do the impossible, Lord. Do so now! Hear my prayer. Help me overcome any unbelief I may have. And I will leave all the results to You. In Your name I pray, amen.

"Have mercy on us and help us, if you can." "What do you mean, 'If I can'?" Jesus asked. "Anything is possible if a person believes." The father instantly cried out, "I do believe, but help me overcome my unbelief!" . . . Jesus. . .rebuked the evil spirit. . . . The boy appeared to be dead. . . . But Jesus took him by the hand and helped him to his feet, and he stood up.
MARK 9:22–27 NLT

Day 289

Calm My Anxious Fears

God, sometimes my fears swell inside of me like a surging tide, threatening to overwhelm me with deep waters. Life seems dark, frightening, and uncertain—teetering on a razor's edge. I don't know how the world can face another day without You, Father.

When I am afraid, I come to You for peace, hope, protection, and love. You have promised never to leave my side. Help me to remember that prayer and thanksgiving are the antidotes to my anxious fears. Wash my mind in Your peace that is beyond understanding. Bolster me with an attitude of power and love, because You are able, You have called me by name, and I belong to You. I walk in the power of Your Spirit . . .whom shall I fear? Amen.

For God has not given us a spirit of fear and timidity,
but of power, love, and self-discipline.
2 Timothy 1:7 nlt

Day 290
Beautiful Plans

Dear God, I realize I don't need to stress out about what comes next. I get to dream and hope all I want, trusting that You know the desire of my heart and that it will come to pass if it's Your will. This knowledge takes pressure off me to perform. I don't have to wring my hands, hoping I can make some headway with my dreams. Before I was born, You numbered my days. You know every step I'll take before I see You face-to-face. So I choose not to be afraid of missing out or messing up. Instead, I'll make beautiful plans and trust You'll bring them to fruition if it's Your perfect will. In Jesus' name I pray, amen.

It would be best to say, "If it is the Lord's will and we live long enough, we hope to do this project or pursue that dream."
JAMES 4:15 VOICE

Day 291

God Gives You Rest

Lord, when I feel all alone, wondering how I will ever do what You have called me to do, remind me that You are with me. That Your actual presence is within my reach. That the steps I take You are taking right along with me. And that along this road, this pathway that we walk together, You will give me the rest I need.

You know my name, Lord. You know everything about me—my past and my future, my heartaches and joys, my loves and losses. You know me like no other. Help me to know You just as well, Lord. All so that I may know how best to please You. Amen.

Moses said to the LORD, "See, you say to me, 'Bring up this people,' but you have not let me know whom you will send with me. Yet you have said, 'I know you by name, and you have also found favor in my sight.' Now therefore. . .please show me now your ways, that I may know you in order to find favor in your sight. . . ." And he said, "My presence will go with you, and I will give you rest."
EXODUS 33:12–14 ESV

Day 292

He Can

Lord Jesus, the world says that You were just a man—a charismatic teacher who rattled the status quo and forged unforgettable history. But my heart cries out that there's so much more to Your story. That You were no mere mortal. My heart sings with the knowledge that You didn't stay in that grave!

I believe, Jesus, that You are God's beloved Son, the Godman who walked blamelessly and died in my place to rise again and be seated beside the throne of God. My heart shouts as Mary did to the disciples three days after the horror of Your death—Jesus is alive! Lord, crush every doubt and let me live each moment in the breathtaking power of belief. Amen.

"Have mercy on us and help us, if you can." "What do you mean, 'If I can'?" Jesus asked. "Anything is possible if a person believes."
MARK 9:22–23 NLT

Day 293

Don't Be Impressed

Dear God, keep me from being jealous of those who have more than me. Even though it's hard to watch them live what I consider an easy life, I have no idea what's happening behind closed doors. They may be miserable in their marriage, have unhealed pain, struggle with addictions, or completely hate their life. I need to focus on being the best me and living in gratitude for what I've been given. At the root of my envious feelings is fear that I'm not as good as they are. I worry I'll never measure up. But the truth is I'm not supposed to find my worth by comparing myself to others. Remind me I'm valuable simply because I'm Yours. In Jesus' name I pray, amen.

So don't be impressed with those who get rich and pile up fame and fortune. They can't take it with them; fame and fortune all get left behind.
PSALM 49:16–17 MSG

Day 294

Mountainous Faith

Lord, today I put all things—all my worries, concerns, plans, ideas, dreams, hopes, and aspirations and my whole self—into Your hands. I am determined to have constant faith in You.

You know all the obstacles that lie before me, Lord. You know the mountains I cannot get over, under, or around. Yet because of You and Your power, I know these hurdles will not remain here, blocking my path. I have no doubt in my heart that You will remove them for me because I am asking You to. I believe in Your mountain-moving power. And I have peace in my life, Lord, knowing there is nothing that You, my mighty God, cannot do. In Jesus' name, amen.

*Jesus, replying, said to them, Have faith in God [constantly].
Truly I tell you, whoever says to this mountain, Be lifted
up and thrown into the sea! and does not doubt at all in
his heart but believes that what he says will take place,
it will be done for him. For this reason I am telling you,
whatever you ask for in prayer, believe (trust and be
confident) that it is granted to you, and you will [get it].*

MARK 11:22–24 AMPC

Day 295

Beware the Enemy

Lord, You warn us to be alert because our enemy, the devil, prowls around like a lion looking for someone to devour. The saying "know your enemy" holds true to my Christian walk as well. Satan wants only to steal and kill and destroy. And he lies. I need to know his tricks inside and out so I don't fall prey to his wiles. He's been lying from the beginning of time.

Thank You, God, that I can always tell when Satan tries to lie to me because my thoughts won't match what You say to me in Your Word. Keep me vigilant. I praise You, Father, for always speaking truth to me. I know that I can trust Your words without a doubt. Amen.

"For there is no truth in [the devil]. When he lies, he speaks his native language, for he is a liar and the father of lies."
JOHN 8:44 NIV

Day 296

The Hard Things

Dear God, help me be effective for what's ahead. I already feel the struggle, for the battle will most certainly be uphill. I have amazing support from friends and family, but I need You most of all. I am scared because there's much at stake and I don't want to make the wrong choices. I know that when I feel weak, You will make me strong. When I'm confused, You will bring wisdom. In those times when I'm overrun with worry, I can always find peace through You. Today, I am asking for all those things. Thank You for being a hands-on God who promises never to leave us alone to figure things out. In Jesus' name I pray, amen.

Give us help for the hard task; human help is worthless.
In God we'll do our very best; he'll flatten the opposition for good.
PSALM 60:11–12 MSG

Day 297

Discernment for Truth

Dear God, give me discernment to see the truth. Sometimes it's easy to follow the rabbit trail of conspiracy theories because it gives me space to ruminate about situations, trying to connect dots. It can remove the blame from me and put it other places or on other people. But it also has a way of destabilizing me and conjuring up fear. I don't need my thoughts running a million miles in the wrong direction. Instead, I need a clear mind to find the truth. I need to trust You to clear the fog of confusion. And I don't want to sit in unnecessary fear over something that's baseless. I know that's not Your will for me. In Jesus' name I pray, amen.

"Don't be like this people, always afraid somebody is plotting against them. Don't fear what they fear. Don't take on their worries."
ISAIAH 8:12 MSG

Day 298

Greater Purpose

God, I have been drifting through my days on a steady diet of anxiety—trying to keep up appearances, keep up with the Joneses, and. . .well, just keeping up. But my life has been infused with new purpose now. I no longer wander this world wondering what it's all about and searching for the point of living.

You've commissioned me into Your army and given me an assignment to fulfill. My mission is to make disciples for You—to share the fantastic news of what living a life with You is really like. . .and to live a life that glorifies Your kingdom. I pray that You would keep me from distraction and shield me from the enemy's attacks so I can work faithfully in Your harvest. Amen.

How, then, can they call on the one they have not believed in?
And how can they believe in the one of whom they have not heard?
And how can they hear without someone preaching to them?
And how can anyone preach unless they are sent? As it is written:
"How beautiful are the feet of those who bring good news!"
ROMANS 10:14–15 NIV

Day 299

Cling to God

Dear God, help me guard my eyes so that all I see is truth. There is so much deception in the world today, and I don't want to get caught up in it any longer. I don't want to be easily tricked or misled. In Your goodness, please give me wisdom to know what I'm dealing with and discernment to choose the right path. Keep me from being so set in my ways that I'm unable to consider something different. Don't allow fear to keep me stuck in the wrong narrative. I only want Your truth to rule in my life. I want You to be my North Star. And the only thing I want to cling to is You. In Jesus' name I pray, amen.

*"But instead, you are clinging to lies
and illusions that are worthless."*
JEREMIAH 7:8 VOICE

Day 300

Bitter Juices

There are people I need to forgive, Lord Jesus, but I'm having a hard time doing so. The wounds are either very fresh or very deep. The ironic thing about it is that while I remain stewing in my bitter juices, those I've not yet forgiven are going along their merry way, most likely having completely forgotten about the words or episode that created the divide.

At the same time, I know Father God won't forgive me unless I forgive those who've harmed me. So help me do so now, Lord Jesus. Help me bring all these names, faces, words, and incidents before You, drop them at Your feet, and leave them there, allowing only forgiveness to remain within my heart and upon my lips. In Your name and power I pray, amen.

Whenever you stand praying, if you have anything against anyone, forgive him and let it drop (leave it, let it go), in order that your Father Who is in heaven may also forgive you your [own] failings and shortcomings and let them drop. But if you do not forgive, neither will your Father in heaven forgive your failings and shortcomings.

MARK 11:25–26 AMPC

Day 301

The Sleep of Peace

Some nights I have trouble sleeping, Lord. I have so many worries on my mind. Sometimes I even find it difficult to think, to laugh, to enjoy my life, the life with which You've blessed me.

Help me, Lord, to just look to You and follow Your Word and way. Help me remember that no matter what happens, I'm safe in You. That in You I can find the rest that heals, refreshes, and rejuvenates. Plant Your wisdom in my heart, God of all, so that I can sleep in peace with no cause for fear, knowing You are watching over me, protecting me. You are guarding my steps, making sure I'm on the right path.

In You alone can I sleep the sleep of peace. In Jesus' name I pray, amen.

"If you follow my decrees and are careful to obey my commands, I will send you the seasonal rains. The land will then yield its crops, and the trees of the field will produce their fruit. . . . I will give you peace in the land, and you will be able to sleep with no cause for fear."
LEVITICUS 26:3–4, 6 NLT

Day 302

More Patience, Please

Lord, sometimes when I want something to happen—when I want You to move on my behalf or change someone else's heart—I find myself tapping my foot, checking the time, and wondering what is taking You so long to make some progress.

But, Father, when it comes to my own shortcomings, I'm so very grateful for Your great and measured patience. Your love is so boundless for me that it expresses itself in unhurried patience for my spiritual growth. You don't shove me forward or stomp Your foot at my hardheaded mistakes. Instead You speak in soft whispers and diligently prune me as I grow. Father, increase my patience for other people. My stress will surely decrease as I offer more patience and understanding to the people around me. Amen.

The Lord is not slow in keeping his promise, as some understand slowness. Instead he is patient with you, not wanting anyone to perish, but everyone to come to repentance.

2 PETER 3:9 NIV

Day 303

The Firm Foundation

Dear God, I don't have to be afraid because You are my firm foundation. If I can keep this perspective when the storms of life hit and I get scared, I'll be able to find footing in my faith. At the end of the day, You're all I have anyway. You are the constant—the one who never changes. So when my world feels chaotic and confusing, I can always cling to You to steady me. There is no fear too big, no problem too complex, no worry too weighty, and no insecurity too tangled for You. Help me remember to turn to You first. And be quick to catch me when I fall. In Jesus' name I pray, amen.

The fundamental fact of existence is that this trust in God, this faith, is the firm foundation under everything that makes life worth living. It's our handle on what we can't see. The act of faith is what distinguished our ancestors, set them above the crowd.
HEBREWS 11:1–2 MSG

Day 304

Unseen and Eternal

Lord, I refuse to worry or panic about things over which I have no control. For I don't want—and was not designed—to live a life consumed by fretfulness over every little thing, including my age.

I realize that with each passing day my outer self, my outer woman, is aging. For that is the way of nature. Yet the spiritual is a vastly different matter. Although my outer woman may have a few gray hairs, my inner woman is being renewed each day. For You are preparing me for a much grander and more wonderful place.

Thus, I will keep my eyes on the unseen rather than the seen, knowing that what I can see is fading away, but what is unseen will last forever. Amen.

So we do not lose heart. Though our outer self is wasting away, our inner self is being renewed day by day. For this light momentary affliction is preparing for us an eternal weight of glory beyond all comparison, as we look not to the things that are seen but to the things that are unseen. For the things that are seen are transient, but the things that are unseen are eternal.

2 CORINTHIANS 4:16–18 ESV

Day 305

The King of All

Lord, I think we all sometimes indulge in the fantasy of being queen for a day. The perks sound appealing. Who wouldn't be enamored with an unlimited budget, people to see to my every need, and all the coffee and chocolate I could want resting at my fingertips?

But as I imagine being in charge of everything, making weighty decisions, and bearing the burden of all that control, I can feel my stress levels rising. Father, I'm so thankful that I can relinquish that job to You. You are the sovereign over Your kingdom. You wield all the greatness and power of Your position. And because I trust in the King who rules everything, I can lay all the responsibility for that authority on Your capable shoulders. Amen.

Yours, LORD, is the greatness and the power and the glory and the majesty and the splendor, for everything in heaven and earth is yours. Yours, LORD, is the kingdom; you are exalted as head over all.

1 CHRONICLES 29:11 NIV

Day 306

Ask God to Meet You

Dear God, meet me in my fear and bring it under Your control. I'm paralyzed in it and feel hopeless. I can't find my footing to get up and catch my breath, and I'm worried. I've made a mess of my life, and I'm unable to clean it up. I desperately need You right now. I'm choosing to trust that I'll find peace through Jesus, so I'm taking You up on Your offer of always being available. Please come quickly to stop my anxiety. Cover me in calm. Remind me of Your love. Show me that I matter. And speak encouragement into my spirit. Meet me more than halfway and free me from this debilitating fear. I need You. In Jesus' name I pray, amen.

God met me more than halfway, he freed me from my anxious fears.
PSALM 34:4 MSG

Day 307

Soul to Soul

You and I are linked, Lord, Soul to soul. You have promised to be with me always, to walk beside me and live within me, never to hate, reject, or abandon me.

You have brought me so far, Lord, in this journey of life. From an egg within my mother's womb to my present self, You have led me to Your love, protection, and joy. You have brought me out of the darkness and into Your light. You have made me a free and upright woman, wanting and loving to be with You and to please You. In You, I find the peace, the calm, and the delight I desire. Amen.

I will set My dwelling in and among you, and My soul shall not despise or reject or separate itself from you. And I will walk in and with and among you and will be your God, and you shall be My people. I am the Lord your God, Who brought you forth out of the land of Egypt, that you should no more be slaves; and I have broken the bars of your yoke and made you walk erect [as free men].

LEVITICUS 26:11–13 AMPC

Day 308

Receive Mercy

Heavenly Father, Your limitless mercy is a healing balm to my soul. It soothes my aching fears and kindles hope within me that I haven't strayed too far—that I haven't crossed a point of no return where Your mercy and grace don't reach.

Lord, Your Word says that You desire mercy over sacrifice, life over death. Lead me in the way of mercy, Father, so that in everyday living I can extend Your mercy to others. May I be a beacon of light heralding Your grace and mercy to the world. It's so easy to desire retribution when I am wronged, but I must remember how my sins have drowned in the tides of Your mercy. In the name of Jesus my Savior, amen.

Let us then approach God's throne of grace
with confidence, so that we may receive mercy and
find grace to help us in our time of need.

HEBREWS 4:16 NIV

Day 309

Desperate and Defeated

Dear God, I'm hurting. It feels like so much is going wrong in my life, and I'm worried that things won't get better. It's been a long road—so many years of continued heartbreak—and I'm losing stamina. I've tried being brave, but it didn't last long. I've tried standing up for myself, but I lacked real courage to maintain it. In the end, I'm still here, stuck. Hear my voice and wrap me in Your arms. Don't leave me to figure this out alone. Help me feel safe and secure. I'm feeble and in need of Your deliverance. I'm at the end of me and surrendering every fear to You. Please save me and restore my broken heart. In Jesus' name I pray, amen.

When I had nothing, desperate and defeated,
I cried out to the Lord and he heard me, bringing his
miracle-deliverance when I needed it most.

PSALM 34:6 TPT

Day 310

Sleep Well

If not for You holding my hand, Lord, I would stumble and fall. If not for Your protection, I would lose courage. Continue, Lord, to be the shield that surrounds me, the one who helps me keep my cool no matter what others say about me.

You, Lord, are the only one I can truly depend on, for You answer me when I call. You sweep onto the scene when I am in trouble. Because I know You will never leave or abandon me, I am able to sleep well at night and arise knowing I'm safe, for my tent is pitched in Your camp. My small hand is held in Your larger one. Because You watch over me, I have nothing to fear. Amen.

You, O LORD, are a shield around me; you are my glory, the one who holds my head high. I cried out to the LORD, and he answered me from his holy mountain. . . . I lay down and slept, yet I woke up in safety, for the LORD was watching over me. I am not afraid of ten thousand enemies who surround me on every side. . . . Victory comes from you, O LORD. May you bless your people.
PSALM 3:3–6, 8 NLT

Day 311

God Is So Good!

Dear God, You are so good! I stepped out in faith and trusted You with my fears, and I'm now blessed with peace. I chose to surrender my insecurities, and You grew my confidence. When I admitted my anxiety, it was supernaturally replaced with fearlessness to move forward. How wonderful that You are who You say You are! And how powerful to watch You do what You say You'll do! I am so grateful for Your faithfulness to make good on promises from the Word. What an encouragement to my weary soul to see things in my life shift in such meaningful ways. Thank You for being able and willing to deliver me from bondage. In Jesus' name I pray, amen.

Taste of His goodness; see how wonderful the Eternal truly is.
Anyone who puts trust in Him will be blessed and comforted.
PSALM 34:8 VOICE

Day 312

Flexible

Father, as I age my body is not nearly as flexible as it used to be. But I fear that my attitude also gets less flexible. I'm more set in my ways, less understanding of people whose circumstances don't match up with mine, and so impatient when I don't get my way.

But, Father, I know that a flexible attitude can de-stress my life. Increase my willingness to change my plans whenever it is important—putting the needs and desires of others first is so important! Teach me to be gracious and accepting of interruptions in my life, Lord, and less rigid with the plans I set in my mind so that I don't miss opportunities You put in front of me. Amen.

A servant of the Lord must not quarrel but must be kind to everyone, be able to teach, and be patient with difficult people.
2 TIMOTHY 2:24 NLT

Day 313

In Need of Deliverance

Dear God, I cannot believe this is my life. How did I get here, and will I ever be happy again? Will I ever not be triggered by fear? Will I find deliverance from this chaos? I need You right now, Lord. Bring me out of this dark valley and back into the wide-open spaces full of sunshine. Bless me with courage and confidence to fight on so I don't run away again, scared and hopeless. I want to be healed from this pattern of living. I want to see a new season of life full of freedom. I want to taste and see Your goodness and be encouraged. Hear my cries from this pit and come quickly! In Jesus' name I pray, amen.

When the righteous cry out, the LORD listens; he delivers them from all their troubles. The LORD is close to the brokenhearted; he saves those whose spirits are crushed.
PSALM 34:17–18 CEB

Day 314

Richness in God

I'm not sure people know what to think of me sometimes, Lord. For even though I seem meek, mild, and gentle to them, I have such strength in and from You. That's why I can do the things You have called me to do. So no matter how I am treated by others, I still look to and serve You. And I'm good with that. No matter how much my heart may ache at times, I can always find an abundance of joy in You. I may not have much materially, but I am able to give away what I have in spiritual riches. And although I don't own much of anything, yet in You I have all I need—and so much more! All praise, glory, and honor to You!

God's power is working in us. . . . We serve God whether people honor us or despise us, whether they slander us or praise us. We are honest, but they call us impostors. . . . Our hearts ache, but we always have joy. We are poor, but we give spiritual riches to others. We own nothing, and yet we have everything.
2 Corinthians 6:7–8, 10 nlt

Day 315

Not Alone

Father, I don't like being distant from my family, friends, and job because of sickness. I'm not wired this way; I need social interaction. I need to be close to others. I need hand shaking and hugging; and unfortunately, spending time with others is frowned upon and unwise when we have certain illnesses. Help me to remember that I'm not isolated from You. Father, forgive me for social distancing from You. I've waited until things were looking desperate to call on You. But You long for a relationship with me. Help me to remember all the promises You've already kept, the battles You've already won on my behalf. You have definitely proven Yourself trustworthy. I know that ultimately Jesus wins. All the time. Every time. Even this time. No matter what. Amen.

Where can I go from your Spirit? Where can I flee from your presence? If I go up to the heavens, you are there; if I make my bed in the depths, you are there. If I rise on the wings of the dawn, if I settle on the far side of the sea, even there your hand will guide me, your right hand will hold me fast.

PSALM 139:7–10 NIV

Day 316

Learning to Duck

Dear God, bless me with the wisdom to see trouble coming my way so I can duck. I'm asking for spiritual eyes so I can perceive the situation clearly and avoid being caught off guard all the time. So often I feel exposed and afraid, unprotected in a world where evil is prevalent. Sure, there will be some situations that blow in without warning, but if I am wise and watchful, I'll be able to prepare myself for what's coming. I may not have the ability to prevent it, but I can prepare my heart. Help me live unafraid of the future. By trusting in You, I can have confidence that things will work out. In Jesus' name I pray, amen.

A prudent person sees trouble coming and ducks;
a simpleton walks in blindly and is clobbered.
PROVERBS 27:12 MSG

Day 317

Who Keeps the World Spinning?

God, You are the one who keeps this world spinning. You are the Mighty One who can right all wrongs. You can battle giants, wrestle leviathans, and conquer armies. At the same time, You are the good and gentle shepherd who lovingly calls, guides, and protects Your lambs.

Here I am, Lord. One of Your sheep. I'm in dire straits. I need You now in all Your power and might to defend me, deliver me, protect me, pull me up out of this frenzied fray. Save me from those who have come to trouble me. Make their hands weak, their words powerless. And equip me to say what You would have me say and do what You would have me do to honor You. Amen.

The Mighty One, God, the Lord, speaks and calls the earth from the rising of the sun to its setting. . . . The heavens declare His righteousness (rightness and justice), for God, He is judge. Selah [pause, and calmly think of that]! Hear, O My people, and I will speak. . . . Call on Me in the day of trouble; I will deliver you, and you shall honor and glorify Me.

Psalm 50:1, 6–7, 15 ampc

Day 318

Faith Walk

Lord, the world says that faith is blind. But I know my eyes can deceive me by what I'm unable to see. My faith eyes recognize that this world is not all there is to life. My trust in the things I'm hoping for—those wonderful things I know are waiting for me in eternity, but I can't yet see in the here and now—keeps me going through the hard times and gives my faith something to grab on to in my most difficult seasons.

God, my long, intimate journey with You has given me all the evidence I need that You are trustworthy. God, keep my eyes of faith open wide. I want to confidently follow You, knowing every word You have spoken is concrete truth. Amen.

So we are always confident and know that while we are at home in the body we are away from the Lord. For we walk by faith, not by sight. In fact, we are confident, and we would prefer to be away from the body and at home with the Lord. Therefore, whether we are at home or away, we make it our aim to be pleasing to him.

2 CORINTHIANS 5:6–9 CSB

Day 319

A Gift?

Dear God, it's challenging for me to see hard seasons as a gift. It feels counterintuitive, considering how I feel most of the time. When I'm sitting in fear and insecurity, being joyful isn't usually my first response. Too often, I give in to the negative thoughts. I let the feelings of hopelessness win. Lord, I need Your strength to keep me engaged in the battle. I need confidence to stay in the moment rather than look for an escape route. I need bold faith to believe You are in the details. Help me trust that You allowed this fearful season only because it will help grow my faith. And give me the courage to stand. In Jesus' name I pray, amen.

Consider it a sheer gift, friends, when tests and challenges come at you from all sides. You know that under pressure, your faith-life is forced into the open and shows its true colors. So don't try to get out of anything prematurely. Let it do its work so you become mature and well-developed, not deficient in any way.

JAMES 1:2–4 MSG

Day 320

Found

Thank You, Lord, for always keeping Your eye out for me, no matter how far I've strayed. You're always opening Your arms to me, pulling me into Your embrace, kissing me, loving me. You barely even listen to my sad apology, the speech I have practiced over and over again, the one in which I tell You how much I have misstepped. How You no longer even have to call me Your daughter. Instead, seeing me back home, once more before You, You are calling out commands, saying that I should be honored because I was lost but now am found. Oh, what love You have for Your children, Father! Amen.

*"When he was still a long way off, his father saw him.
His heart pounding, he ran out, embraced him, and kissed him.
The son started his speech: 'Father, I've sinned against God,
I've sinned before you; I don't deserve to be called your son
ever again.' But the father wasn't listening. He was calling to
the servants, 'Quick. Bring a clean set of clothes and dress him.
Put the family ring on his finger and sandals on his feet.'"*
LUKE 15:20–22 MSG

Day 321

No Shadow of Shame

Jesus, I've done things that I'm not proud of. Shame stains my life, and crimson blooms on my cheeks. My sins condemn me like the angry religious leaders who threatened to stone a woman caught in adultery. They hurled accusations like rocks and condemned her to a horrible and pain-filled death. And my sentence was the same.

But I have hope because You didn't condemn her, Jesus. Instead, You stepped into the circle of their accusations with her, and You forgave her. Just as You have forgiven me. Thank You, Jesus, that You've wiped away my shame and replaced it with the joy of knowing Your grace and mercy. I am clean! To the question, "Have you no shame?" I can shout, "No!" In the precious name of Jesus, amen.

Those who look to him for help will be radiant with joy; no shadow of shame will darken their faces.

PSALM 34:5 NLT

Day 322

Bold Enough to Ask

Dear God, I confess that I'm scared to ask You for certain things. Not all things, just some. The reason is that they feel trivial or unimportant. In the grand scheme of things, these requests seem silly. They feel either too big or too out there. And I don't want to bog You down with ask after ask. Help me remember I don't exhaust You. Remind me You want to hear what's on my heart. And make me brave enough to put any request before You with confidence. Even more, help me trust that however and whenever You choose to answer me is always for my benefit and Your glory, so I can be grateful no matter what. In Jesus' name I pray, amen.

"Until now you've not been bold enough to ask the Father
for a single thing in my name, but now you can ask,
and keep on asking him! And you can be sure that you'll
receive what you ask for, and your joy will have no limits!"
JOHN 16:24 TPT

Day 323

Stand in Awe

I've got no worries today, Lord, because I have Your Word. And if I have any questions, if I need peace, if I need help, if I need love, all I need to do is come to You and ask that You would show me the answers I'm searching for and provide the calm I crave, the help I need, and the love I long for.

Lord, before You and Your power, I stand in awe. For nothing is here that You have not made. You speak, and things that never existed become reality. You command, and things just are. Because of You, I am! Amen.

For the word of the LORD is right, and all His work is trustworthy. He loves righteousness and justice; the earth is full of the LORD's unfailing love. . . . Let the whole earth tremble before the LORD; let all the inhabitants of the world stand in awe of Him. For He spoke, and it came into being; He commanded, and it came into existence. . . . The counsel of the LORD stands forever, the plans of His heart from generation to generation.
PSALM 33:4–5, 8–9, 11 HCSB

Day 324

A Beautiful Life

Dear God, I want everything You planned for my life. I'm full of hope and energy, ready to live out my days with purpose and passion. My heart is full of determination to have my life reflect Your goodness. But sometimes fear gets in the way. I worry I might make a wrong choice or run out of steam. What if I let others down? More importantly, what if I let You down? Help me take a step back so I don't run ahead of You, and give me the spiritual eyes and ears to follow Your lead. I know that with my willingness and Your favor, I can live a beautiful life that makes a difference. In Jesus' name I pray, amen.

Instead, You direct me on the path that leads to a beautiful life. As I walk with You, the pleasures are never-ending, and I know true joy and contentment.
PSALM 16:11 VOICE

Day 325

One Step at a Time

God, I'm overwhelmed by this gargantuan task I'm faced with. When I look at it in its entirety, I feel defeated at the onset. It's like trying to run a marathon after training for one week while downing chocolate cake every day. I'm not sure I can see a way to get it done, and that stresses me out.

Help me to lean on You, Father—on Your wisdom and Your strength—for the job I have to finish. Show me how to put one foot in front of the other. Teach me to break it down into smaller, more manageable goals. And then give me energy and focus to start working on those goals. I know that if I can think of things in smaller chunks, I can make progress. Amen.

All hard work brings a profit, but mere talk leads only to poverty.
PROVERBS 14:23 NIV

Day 326

Truest Friend

I have many acquaintances, Lord, but I have few close friends, ones who I know will stick by me through thick and thin. Yet without a doubt my truest, most loving friend is You, Lord. Only You loved me so much that You laid down Your life for me—and that was before I even came into being! Your great love boggles my mind and moves my heart.

Yet what I love even more is that You have claimed me as Your friend—again, before I even knew You. And all I have to do to honor that friendship is to obey You, to do what is right in Your eyes. Help me to honor You in that way every day, Lord, for You are my truest friend.

There are "friends" who destroy each other, but a real friend sticks closer than a brother. . . . "There is no greater love than to lay down one's life for one's friends. You are my friends if you do what I command. I no longer call you slaves, because a master doesn't confide in his slaves. Now you are my friends."
PROVERBS 18:24; JOHN 15:13–15 NLT

Day 327

Celebrating God

Dear God, forgive me for all the times I've doubted You. Too often, I've found myself worrying that You aren't going to show up in my stressful situation. I've told myself You're too busy with bigger issues to listen to mine. I've wondered if You get tired of hearing the same frustrations and fears from me over and over again. And without my wanting it to, that mindset ends up shutting me down and shutting me up. I'm sorry for letting anxiety and insecurity come between us. Help cultivate in me a heart of joy and gladness. Let me enjoy our relationship! Open my eyes to the ways You're working in my life, and let's celebrate Your kindness and faithfulness! In Jesus' name I pray, amen.

This is the very day GOD acted—let's celebrate and be festive!
PSALM 118:24 MSG

Day 328

Simplify

Father God, I'm so overwhelmed. I've lost count of the number of times I've wished to clone myself. Not because I want a copy of myself scurrying around, but because I need help. I'm not sure I can straighten out all the details and finish all the to-do lists that clutter my plate. But maybe my harried attitude is a warning sign.

You said that You bring peace. So maybe Your expectations for my time aren't as high as the ones I've made for myself. Maybe You're asking me to be still for a while. Father, please help me to simplify my life. Show me what matters to You. And fill me with the supernatural help of the Holy Spirit to accomplish those things that are on Your list. Amen.

Make it your ambition to lead a quiet life: You should mind your own business and work with your hands, just as we told you.

1 THESSALONIANS 4:11 NIV

Day 329

Worried for Joy

Dear God, sometimes I worry that I'll never find joy again. This season of life has been so difficult that I'm fearful happiness will always elude me. There doesn't seem to be anything worth hoping for, especially because my heart can't handle being let down again. I'm struggling to find my happy place right now. So I'm thankful for the reminder that You are the joy giver. No matter what the world may offer as a short-term solution, You promise to fill me with lasting joy even in the toughest times. It's through Your goodness that I can be fulfilled, feeling whole in heart again. You're the one who will make joy overflow into the good times and the tough seasons. In Jesus' name I pray, amen.

The intense pleasure you give me surpasses the gladness of harvest time, even more than when the harvesters gaze upon their ripened grain and when their new wine overflows.

PSALM 4:7 TPT

Day 330

Surprised by Love

When I am drowning in my sorrows, problems, unanswered questions, worries, and what-ifs, You come along and save me, Lord. Even when others might kick me when I'm down, You are there with me, standing immovable, right by my side.

Thank You, God, for sticking by me. For pulling me up out of the deep waters where I cannot save myself. For getting me out of jams and setting me down in wide-open spaces where I can breathe once more and stand there safe, amazed that You love me like no one else ever could. Amen.

> GOD roared in protest, let loose his hurricane anger.
> But me he caught—reached all the way from sky to sea;
> he pulled me out of that ocean of hate, that enemy chaos,
> the void in which I was drowning. They hit me when I was
> down, but GOD stuck by me. He stood me up on a wide-
> open field; I stood there saved—surprised to be loved!
>
> 2 SAMUEL 22:16–20 MSG

Day 331

His Arms Are Always Open

Dear God, when I really mess up, I worry about being rejected by those that matter to me. I start obsessing about what they will think of my bad choices. I worry about being judged and criticized in hurtful ways. It scares me. But in Your steadfast love for me, I'm always welcomed with open arms. Thank You for not holding my imperfections against me. I appreciate that Your heart for me is always good and not dependent on me being flawless. And I'm so grateful that my wrong decisions and weak choices don't scare You away and that I can't sin enough to turn You off. That in and of itself is worthy of celebration! In Jesus' name I pray, amen.

But you'll welcome us with open arms when we run
for cover to you. Let the party last all night! Stand
guard over our celebration. You are famous, GOD, for
welcoming God-seekers, for decking us out in delight.
PSALM 5:11–12 MSG

Day 332

Taste His Goodness

Father, I believe that You are good, even in the midst of this stressful season. Thank You for inviting me to taste just how good You are. Just as I roll a new food around in my mouth to investigate all of its intricate flavors, You bid me to experience every facet of Your personality and discover the sweet, delicate flavor of Your excellent goodness.

When I look for Your good workings around me, my perspective alters. I see You changing lives, bringing peace, healing hurts. Even though tragic and terrible things are happening in this world, I know that Your far-reaching gaze sees both the beginning and the end and that Your true flavor is one of complexity and layers. Serve another portion of Your exquisite goodness to this world today. Amen.

Taste and see that the LORD is good; blessed
is the one who takes refuge in him.

PSALM 34:8 NIV

Day 333

The God Who Comforts

Dear God, I love that You are such a calming force in my life. When my relationships feel chaotic, You are quick to bring my heart into alignment. You're the one to shift expectations when I begin to worry. When the bad news sucker punches me in the gut, it's Your kindness that lets me find rest. You make things feel manageable when stress tries to stir up my emotions. Your love calms my anxieties when they begin to flare. And when peace feels distant, all I have to do is ask for Your help. Thank You for knowing the value and importance of bringing comfort. I'm so blessed by the reassurance You so generously give. In Jesus' name I pray, amen.

When my anxieties multiply, your comforting calms me down.
PSALM 94:19 CEB

Day 334

In His Name

This promise is so hard to believe, Lord Jesus. That if I have faith in You, I can do the same works here on earth that You have done—or perhaps even greater works! Yet that is the truth You have laid at my door. That is what is written in Your Word.

You continually surprise me. For You, Lord, are always doing the unbelievable, the seemingly impossible. And all You ask of me is to believe, to have faith in who You are and what You can do.

So here I am, Lord, asking something in Your name. And I am believing that, if it's according to Your will, it is something You will do. All so that You can bring glory to our Father! That's something we both can celebrate. In Your name, amen. Amen!

"I tell you the truth, anyone who believes in me will do the same works I have done, and even greater works, because I am going to be with the Father. You can ask for anything in my name, and I will do it, so that the Son can bring glory to the Father. Yes, ask me for anything in my name, and I will do it!"
JOHN 14:12–14 NLT

Day 335

Supernatural Solutions

God, I live in breathless awe of You. When the stresses of this life creep over me, I only need to remember that You are no mere man. I cannot measure You in human standards, and the vast depth of this universe cannot contain You. . .and yet You choose to live among us. You choose to take up residence in me. You spoke, and a universe exploded into being. I can't think of a more concentrated power.

When I feel alone, I need only to remember that You live with me. The limitations I see around me have no restraining power over You. When I feel despair because I can't see a way through the tough times, remind me that You are the Mighty One in possession of supernatural power. Amen.

I am God and not a mere mortal. I am the
Holy One living among you.
HOSEA 11:9 NLT

Day 336

He Is the Champion

Dear God, please rescue me. Be my champion. Give me hope that I can overcome the debilitating fear that plagues me. I'm worried about many things right now—things that matter greatly to me. I have anxiety about how everything will work out. I'm concerned that I'll be stuck in this place forever. I've tried so many things to lessen the stress, but I can't seem to find the relief I need. Lord, please intervene. I want to feel Your goodness and delight. Let me hear Your voice over all the others. Bring a sense of peace to my fears so they melt away. But most of all, please fill my heart with joy in knowing You're with me. In Jesus' name I pray, amen.

The Eternal your God is standing right here among you, and
He is the champion who will rescue you. He will joyfully
celebrate over you; He will rest in His love for you;
He will joyfully sing because of you like a new husband.
ZEPHANIAH 3:17 VOICE

Day 337

As Good as Done

Lord, I hate to panic. Yet causes for panic seem to crop up so frequently these days. When some unexpected trouble strikes, uneasiness wells up within me. The next thing I know, my mind is imagining all kinds of wild scenarios. My heart starts beating faster, my breath starts coming more quickly, and there I am—in full-blown panic mode!

So at the first sign of trouble, Lord, prompt my heart and spirit to seek Yours, to tell You what is happening. Then send me a word from You. For I know that as You give a command, it's as good as done. In Your name, amen.

A Roman captain came up in a panic and said, "Master,
my servant is sick. He can't walk. He's in terrible pain."
Jesus said, "I'll come and heal him." "Oh, no," said the captain.
"I don't want to put you to all that trouble. Just give the order
and my servant will be fine. I'm a man who takes orders and
gives orders. I tell one soldier, 'Go,' and he goes; to another,
'Come,' and he comes; to my slave, 'Do this,' and he does it."
MATTHEW 8:5–9 MSG

Day 338

Pursue Holiness

Father God, I want to be Your obedient child. But sometimes I struggle. I slip and fall—I sin. I know that my sins only bring me stress and pain because I'm not doing the things You say are right. Instead I'm going my own way and choosing wrong. Or I'm refusing to break the habits of sin that I've fallen into.

Father, help me to practice being holy. Help me to go back and give myself a "do-over" when I mess up. Sometimes doing the right thing takes practice. And, Father, help me to love lavishly. Scripture tells me that You are love. So I know that unless I am loving lavishly, I am not being holy. Show me how I can pursue holiness this week. Amen.

As obedient children, do not conform to the evil desires
you had when you lived in ignorance. But just as he
who called you is holy, so be holy in all you do; for
it is written: "Be holy, because I am holy."

1 PETER 1:14–16 NIV

Day 339

The God Who Shows Up

Dear God, sometimes I need a reminder that since You showed up for me before, You will do it again. That's not a hope; it's a promise You've made that means so much to me. In hard times, it's important that I think back over all the ways You made something wrong very right. It's powerful when I'm able to remember situations where You rescued me from the enemy's traps. Lord, please bless me with a supernatural memory to recall Your power and mercy in my life. Let the memories strengthen my belief. Let them mature my faith. And use them to encourage me to be patient as I wait for Your hand to move in the difficult times. In Jesus' name I pray, amen.

And now, GOD, do it again—bring rains to our drought-stricken lives so those who planted their crops in despair will shout "Yes!" at the harvest, so those who went off with heavy hearts will come home laughing, with armloads of blessing.
PSALM 126:4–6 MSG

Day 340

Restored and Complete

God, You have known me all of my life. You know when I have fallen apart, when I've brought the pieces of myself before You and allowed You to restore me, to make me the woman You originally created me to be. Then, when I was complete once more, You gave me a fresh start in life. Ever since then, I've looked to You and followed Your way. I've tried not to miss any opportunity You put before me to obey You and keep myself out of trouble. Because of my desire to serve You, to live for You, to lay my heart open before You, You have rewarded me. And all I have left to do is praise Your name! Amen.

GOD made my life complete when I placed all the pieces before him. When I cleaned up my act, he gave me a fresh start. Indeed, I've kept alert to GOD's ways; I haven't taken God for granted. Every day I review the ways he works, I try not to miss a trick. I feel put back together, and I'm watching my step. GOD rewrote the text of my life when I opened the book of my heart to his eyes.
2 SAMUEL 22:21–25 MSG

Day 341

Seeing Clearly

Lord, when I take off my glasses, I'm pretty much blind. The world is a smear of colors with a disturbing lack of details. I fear I'm looking at life in this same manner right now. I've lost my perspective. My faith feels blurry and unsteady, my focus not quite right.

When something bad happens or things don't go my way, I've been letting it ruin my day—and sometimes my week. One negative comment from a friend, one difficult attitude from a child. . .are like ice water sheeting down my spine, bringing out the worst in me. But I know that I can bring things back into focus by putting back on my spiritual glasses and seeing things through the lens of Your Word. Help me see more clearly today. Amen.

"Then you will know the truth, and the truth will set you free."
JOHN 8:32 NIV

Day 342

He Is on the Job

Dear God, forgive me for all the times I've questioned where You were in my situation. I'm sorry that my default response has been to think You've abandoned me. The Word is crystal clear that I am never alone, because Your glorious presence is steadfast and constant. You never walk away from me, be it good or tough times. So rather than let fear take root, may I be strong. Help me understand the privilege of hard seasons as they work to mature my faith. Even more, remind me it's an honor to experience some of what Jesus did while on earth. I'm resolved not to become afraid when my circumstances get messy because I know You are on the job. In Jesus' name I pray, amen.

Friends, when life gets really difficult, don't jump to the conclusion that God isn't on the job. Instead, be glad that you are in the very thick of what Christ experienced. This is a spiritual refining process, with glory just around the corner.
1 PETER 4:12–13 MSG

Day 343

Marvelous Believer

I trust You, Lord, with all things. I have faith that You will do what You say, that You will come through as promised. I may not have grown up believing You as I do now, but having read Your Book and seen Your power at work in the lives of others, I now know that You are the true authority, the master of all things, the beginning and the end, my creator, beloved, healer, and friend. No one and nothing compares to You.

And because of my great faith in You, I know that through You, what I believe can happen will happen. In Your name, amen.

> *Taken aback, Jesus said, "I've yet to come across this kind of simple trust in Israel, the very people who are supposed to know all about God and how he works. This man is the vanguard of many outsiders who will soon be coming from all directions. . . ." Then Jesus turned to the captain and said, "Go. What you believed could happen has happened." At that moment his servant became well.*
> MATTHEW 8:10–11, 13 MSG

Day 344

After You

Father, I can't seem to get out of my own head today. I'm grumpy and stressed and maybe just a teeny bit negative and irritable. . .okay, maybe I'm more like a grizzly who woke up from her long winter nap to a stomach growling louder than she was. You already know the state of my surly mind.

Help me to get off the topic of me and focus outwardly on others. How can I outdo someone in kindness and consideration? How can I show a "you first" attitude? Holy Spirit, nudge me in the direction of honoring others above myself. I know that my attitude will turn around fast when I'm no longer laser-focused on me. Amen.

Love one another deeply as brothers and sisters.
Take the lead in honoring one another.
ROMANS 12:10 CSB

Day 345

Rejoice Instead

Dear God, every time I'm struggling with fear or frustration, I will choose to give You praise. Rather than sit in those unproductive feelings and feel worried for another second, I am going to lift up my voice and rejoice that You are good! The truth is I'm tired of feeling defeated. It's exhausting to always be in an emotional crisis and anxious about the outcome. So from today forward, I will focus solely on Your promises to save and will believe that You're already at work in my stressful situation. I'm not a helpless victim. Because of You, I am not a weak or inferior woman. And starting right now, my loud faith will make sure everyone knows it. In Jesus' name I pray, amen.

*Lift up a great shout of joy to Yahweh! Go ahead
and do it—everyone, everywhere!*
Psalm 100:1 TPT

Day 346

Reminders

Lord, when I am overwhelmed with fear and sadness, remind me who You are. Tell me once more that through You, I can find the courage to do what You prompt me to do. That because You are in my life, I need not be sad. For You can make miracles out of misery and turn troubles into triumph.

Most of all, Lord, remind me of the power of prayer, anytime and anywhere. For prayer is not just for those quiet moments alone when I have time to think things out and find my way into Your presence but also for those times when I need on-the-spot help, when I need to send up a quick arrow prayer to You before I open my mouth. Remind me, Lord, of all the benefits of trusting in You. Amen.

The king said to me, "Why are you sad, when you aren't sick? . . ."
I was overwhelmed with fear and replied to the king, "May the
king live forever! Why should I not be sad when the city where my
ancestors are buried lies in ruins and its gates have been destroyed
by fire?" Then the king asked me, "What is your request?"
So I prayed to the God of heaven and answered the king.
NEHEMIAH 2:2–5 HCSB

Day 347

How Praying and Celebrating Helps

Dear God, whether in fearful times or courageous moments, I will put a priority on growing my relationship with You. I'm fully aware of how desperately I need Your courage, wisdom, and strength in my life every day. I need Your gentle guidance for the next steps as I try to navigate the curveballs that come my way. Thank You for helping me—even if I'm still struggling with a bit of fear. Thank You for the freedom to place my requests before You. I simply cannot walk through life without You! Help me be joyous no matter what. Encourage my heart to celebrate Your goodness and faithfulness. And let my testimony always point to You. In Jesus' name I pray, amen.

Celebrate always, pray constantly, and give thanks to God
no matter what circumstances you find yourself in.
1 Thessalonians 5:16–18 voice

Day 348

The Right Pursuits

God, I love rewards, achievements, and winning—even if there's no prize, I still own the bragging rights. But I have learned through Your Word that my efforts are wasted if I'm striving toward the wrong goals, if I win my prize only to discover that its profits are empty and meaningless in the lens of my eternity. I know the rewards I earn working in Your kingdom won't disappoint me, God, because they offer everlasting returns.

Help me to keep my eyes fixed on Your kingdom, Jesus. This world offers much, but it cannot give me eternity, nor does it deal in the currency of peace and hope. May I run my race well and win the ultimate prize—eternal life in Your great kingdom. . .with You. In the name of Jesus, amen.

Each one's work will become obvious. For the day will disclose it, because it will be revealed by fire; the fire will test the quality of each one's work. If anyone's work that he has built survives, he will receive a reward.

1 Corinthians 3:13–14 csb

Day 349

Listen and Learn

Dear God, give me courage to listen to the advice of others. Let me have an open heart and mind to those who care for me and want the best. It's hard to hear truth sometimes, and there's often shame attached to receiving it. But I know if I can humble myself and trust You, what's shared could be life giving. So please give me a willing heart to learn from the wisdom of others. Let me be open to accepting their words. And surround me with people who care enough to be honest and encouraging. In the end, let me be remembered as one unafraid to listen and learn—and for how that act of humility made my life sweeter. In Jesus' name I pray, amen.

Listen well to wise counsel and be willing to learn from correction
so that by the end of your life you'll be known for your wisdom.
PROVERBS 19:20 TPT

Day 350

Parting Gifts

Lord, because I love You, my desire is to obey Your commands. Yet I need Your help to obey. That's why I am so grateful You left Your peace of mind and heart for me. And that our Father has gifted me with an advocate who not only will teach me what I need to know and remind me of all You have told me but also will never leave me.

Both parting gifts are very much needed to keep me on the right track, Lord, to keep me going in Your will and Your way. Thank You for such precious presents. Because of Your peace and Your Spirit, I can rest assured that I need never be troubled or afraid. In Your name I pray, amen.

"If you love me, obey my commandments. And I will ask the Father, and he will give you another Advocate, who will never leave you." . . . *"The Holy Spirit. . .will teach you everything and will remind you of everything I have told you. I am leaving you with a gift—peace of mind and heart. And the peace I give is a gift the world cannot give. So don't be troubled or afraid."*
JOHN 14:15–16, 26–27 NLT

Day 351

Wait for Him

Lord, I'm experiencing both expectancy and doubt. I have become weary waiting for relief and wondering if this place of distress is where I will remain. Forgive me, Lord, for my faint heart when I become impatient waiting for You. I know You are here and You hear my pleas, but my flesh is weak.

Father, strengthen me with patience and a joyful heart in the face of adversity so I may give witness of You. Give me strength and courage each day as I need it. My peace is in You as the Holy Spirit walks before me each day, leading the way. And as the watchman is sure of the sunrise, I too am sure that You hear my cries. All things are for Your glory and my good. Amen.

I pray to GOD—my life a prayer—and wait for what he'll say and do. My life's on the line before God, my Lord, waiting and watching till morning.
PSALM 130:5–6 MSG

Day 352

Numbered Days

Dear God, I don't want to waste a day worrying about things in my life. I don't want to be so overwhelmed with my own mess that I hide from community. Give me the wisdom to know when I need to focus on me and when I need to focus my time and effort on others, because sometimes I get it wrong. Before I was born, You determined my life. You decided the number of days I would be in the world. You set my path. Help me understand the purpose of my life, and bless me with the ability to walk it out with passion. Remove any fear that may keep me from being intentional in living for You. In Jesus' name I pray, amen.

Help us to remember that our days are numbered, and help
us to interpret our lives correctly. Set your wisdom deeply
in our hearts so that we may accept your correction.
PSALM 90:12 TPT

Day 353

Healer of Broken Hearts

Lord of the brokenhearted, hear my cry. Mend the wounds that scar my being. Lift me up from the bottom of this pit in which my spirit is mired. Deliver me from all my missteps and mistakes. Bind me back together again.

Lord, You know what has crushed my spirit. You know what has driven me down. You know the darkness that has enveloped me. Yet You are the Lord of light. You hold the answer to my plea. Sun of Righteousness with healing in Your wings, fly close to me. Allow Your rays of light to beam down upon me, to warm me, to lift me up and draw me closer to You, where all is well. Amen.

When the righteous cry for help, the Lord hears, and delivers them out of all their distress and troubles. The Lord is close to those who are of a broken heart and saves such as are crushed with sorrow for sin and are humbly and thoroughly penitent. Many evils confront the [consistently] righteous, but the Lord delivers him out of them all. He keeps all his bones; not one of them is broken.
Psalm 34:17–20 ampc

Day 354

God-Given Spirit

Shaper of beings, please reawaken my spirit. Remind me of who You are and what You've had planned for me since the beginning of time. Take away my cowardice, my fears, those insecurities that keep me from doing the things You'd have me do. Infuse my spirit with Your light so that it will be as originally intended by You, a spirit of power, love, calm, sensibility, discipline, and self-control. Then, through the power of Your Holy Spirit whose home is within me, help me guard the truths You have entrusted to me. In Jesus' name I pray, amen.

God did not give us a spirit of timidity (of cowardice, of craven and cringing and fawning fear), but [He has given us a spirit] of power and of love and of calm and well-balanced mind and discipline and self-control. . . . Guard and keep [with the greatest care] the precious and excellently adapted [Truth] which has been entrusted [to you], by the [help of the] Holy Spirit Who makes His home in us.
2 Timothy 1:7, 14 ampc

Day 355

Becoming Righteous

Lord, it's tempting to believe that how I introduce myself to others is what defines me. And if I allow my family, my occupation, or my hobbies to define who I am, they can become the sole factor that people remember about me.

But I know that I have an even more important identity—Your daughter. Because of Jesus' blood, You don't see a sin-stained human when You look at me. Instead, I'm garbed in righteousness. Not because everything I've ever done has been righteous, but because Jesus lived my perfect walk for me. And, Father, because my heart is overflowing from all the good You've poured into my life, I want to go and sin no more too. Help me to live right today. Amen.

God made him who had no sin to be sin for us, so that in him we might become the righteousness of God.
2 CORINTHIANS 5:21 NIV

Day 356

Supernatural Infusion

Dear God, the Word is clear when it says my strength comes from You. It doesn't hint or mince words. It isn't vague, hoping I can decode the truth. No. The Bible straight up says my strength for the battles I face will be supernaturally imparted to me through our relationship. What a huge relief to know that I'll never be too weak. I have no reason to cower. With You, there is no reason to fear because I can't be defeated. As much as I try to figure everything out on my own, the truth remains that You are my source. Please build my confidence in You as I try to live out my life for You every day. In Jesus' name I pray, amen.

Now my beloved ones, I have saved these most important truths for last: Be supernaturally infused with strength through your life-union with the Lord Jesus. Stand victorious with the force of his explosive power flowing in and through you.

EPHESIANS 6:10 TPT

Day 357

Lord of Light

Because like attracts like, Light attracts light. That's why I can connect with You, Lord. For You are close to those who are close to You. You are honest with those who are honest with You. You're good to the good. That's why I'm here, Lord, standing before You. I need the light of Your being to brighten the darkness in which I find myself, for I can't find my way around on my own.

Illuminate the shadows with Your lamp, Lord of light. Flood my pathway with Your being so that I can find my way out of this murky night. Be my shield, my refuge, my ally in this life as I seek Your will and way. In Jesus' name, amen.

You stick by people who stick with you, you're straight with people who're straight with you, you're good to good people, you shrewdly work around the bad ones. You take the side of the down-and-out, but the stuck-up you take down a peg. Suddenly, GOD, your light floods my path, GOD drives out the darkness. . . . What a God! His road stretches straight and smooth. Every GOD-direction is road-tested. Everyone who runs toward him makes it.

2 SAMUEL 22:26–29, 31 MSG

Day 358

Trusting Him Alone

Lord, I'm struggling to see Your plans through my pain. Hurtful circumstances have befallen me. It would be so easy to be angry with You, to cry out and ask why. And I know You are big enough to handle my questions, my inability to understand. You are sovereign and good.

I choose to walk in faith that You haven't abandoned me here in this pain. Through my tears, I trust You. I can see that by removing false supports You also give me the precious gift of learning to trust solely in You. You give me comfort in my devastation, healing through my pain. Even if You choose not to deliver me from these circumstances and I lose something dear to me, still I choose to put my faith in You.

If GOD hadn't been there for me, I never would have made it. The minute I said, "I'm slipping, I'm falling," your love, GOD, took hold and held me fast. When I was upset and beside myself, you calmed me.

PSALM 94:17–19 MSG

Day 359

Placing Full Faith in God

Dear God, in those times when I feel attacked by my enemies, please see me. Let Your eyes be on me when I lack courage to advocate for myself. See my fear increase when I'm intimidated and scared. Be aware of every tear of sadness that streams down my cheeks. Know when I'm worrying and understand the details of my concern. See the confusion and chaos in my path. Help me navigate it all. Lord, I am counting on You to protect me. I am trusting that You will strengthen me for every difficulty. My faith is fully in You, believing You not only see me but also will give me what I need as I press on through life. In Jesus' name I pray, amen.

But the Lord is faithful and will give you strength
and protect you from the evil one.
2 THESSALONIANS 3:3 CEB

Day 360

Look Up, Power Up

Lord of creation, it's hard to imagine how You have formed all the stars I see when I look up to the heavens. You bring them out into the night sky, one by one, calling each by name. Because of Your power and might, not one star is missing or lacks anything.

Just as You name and care for Your celestial beings, You name and care for me. And so You are the one I run to for power when I feel done in. You are the one I go to for strength. For You are my God, my creator, my sustainer, my star-namer! Amen.

Lift up your eyes on high and see! Who has created these? He Who brings out their host by number and calls them all by name; through the greatness of His might and because He is strong in power, not one is missing or lacks anything. . . . He gives power to the faint and weary, and to him who has no might He increases strength [causing it to multiply and making it to abound].
ISAIAH 40:26, 29 AMPC

Day 361

My Supplier

Heavenly Father, please forgive me for prayers that make You sound like a genie in a bottle: "God, today I need. . . I want. . . " Your promise to supply my every need does not mean that I will receive every desire that flits through my discontented mind. Show me where my selfishness has exceeded my generosity.

The Philippian church had been giving sacrificially to support Paul. Have I ever gone without because I gave away something that I wanted or needed? How much stress have I heaped upon myself by trying to get more than I give? Help me to conquer my selfishness and give as generously to others as You have given to me—because You have given more than financial assistance; You have met the needs of my eternal soul. Amen.

And this same God who takes care of me will supply all your needs from his glorious riches, which have been given to us in Christ Jesus. Now all glory to God our Father forever and ever! Amen.
PHILIPPIANS 4:19–20 NLT

Day 362

Be a Climber

Dear God, I don't have to be afraid of anything because You have equipped me to walk out everything that comes at me. Be it a financial fallout or a ruptured relationship, I can stand tall as I follow Your lead through it. No health concern can scare me into giving up. No job loss can make me feel hopeless. As long as I take my worries right to You, my strength won't waver. When I choose to trust You, my faith will breed confidence and courage in my heart. You are the one who gives me what I need to continue on with a positive outlook. And together, we can climb every mountain. In Jesus' name I pray, amen.

The Eternal Lord is my strength! He has made my feet like the feet of a deer; He allows me to walk on high places.
HABAKKUK 3:19 VOICE

Day 363

Open Doors

·Lord of love, give me the courage I need to do what You call me to do. Help me to keep my eyes open and to stay alert. When a door for ministry opens before me, give me boldness to walk through it. Even though others oppose me, give me the moxie to trust in You.

Help me, Lord Jesus, to stand firm in You, to act like a brave woman and be strong—not just physically but spiritually, mentally, and emotionally. Remind me to act in a loving way in all circumstances.

Most of all, Lord, give me the wisdom to take a personal interest in everything that is of You. And to do so with Your grace and love. In Your sweet name I pray, amen.

A wide door for effective ministry has opened for me—yet many
oppose me. . . . Be alert, stand firm in the faith, act like a
man, be strong. Your every action must be done with love. . . .
This greeting is in my own hand—Paul. . . . The grace of the Lord
Jesus be with you. My love be with all of you in Christ Jesus.
1 CORINTHIANS 16:9, 13–14, 21, 23–24 HCSB

Day 364

Journeying with the Lord

I need clear direction, Lord, just like what You gave the Israelites when they were wandering in the wilderness. Remind me to keep my eye out for You, to look for You day and night. To search for where You may already be and to go where You bid me to go. Help me to be very in tune with Your presence, sensing when You're near and going wherever You lead.

Show me, Lord, where You want me to remain and when You want me to move on. For my true desire is to follow Your will and way—day and night. Through every stage of my journey, be a visible presence, glowing so that I can see You in every circumstance. Amen.

Whenever the cloud lifted from the Tabernacle, the people of Israel would set out on their journey, following it. But if the cloud did not rise, they remained where they were until it lifted. The cloud of the LORD hovered over the Tabernacle during the day, and at night fire glowed inside the cloud so the whole family of Israel could see it. This continued throughout all their journeys.

EXODUS 40:36–38 NLT

Day 365

His Best for You

Father, the morning sun unfurls warm fingers across the meadow, coaxing a crowd of decked-out wildflowers to raise their chins and smile into another day. No one plants them and no one waters and nourishes them except You, Father. Their beauty splashes across the summer landscape with unhindered artistic abandon. Tiger lilies and ticklish touch-me-nots, bold butterfly weed and carefree daisies.

You could have given small attention to their creative brushstrokes because, after all, their life is barely a blink; but that's not Your style. Every one is a masterpiece that sings of Your attentive care for every detail. You are the God of the universe who is also the God of each tiny, fleeting flower. Thank You for taking the same care with every detail of my life. Amen.

> *"If God gives such attention to the appearance of wildflowers—
> most of which are never even seen—don't you think he'll attend
> to you, take pride in you, do his best for you? What I'm trying
> to do here is to get you to relax, to not be so preoccupied with
> getting, so you can respond to God's giving. People who don't
> know God and the way he works fuss over these things, but you
> know both God and how he works. Steep your life in God-reality,
> God-initiative, God-provisions. Don't worry about missing out.
> You'll find all your everyday human concerns will be met."*
> MATTHEW 6:30–33 MSG

Scripture Index

THE OLD TESTAMENT

THE NEW TESTAMENT